Second Edition

Ethics through

CHRISTIANITY

for OCR B GCSE Religious Studies

Lorraine Abbott

HODDER
EDUCATION
AN HACHETTE UK COMPANY

Acknowledgements

I would like to thank all those people who have been involved in the writing of this book. Everyone who has provided a personal account of their faith has, I hope, helped to bring a greater sense of life and reality to the students who will use it. The hours spent on the text were only possible through superb family support particularly from Mark, my mum and dad. Encouragement from some great friends and colleagues has been much needed at times and always truly valued: Em, Cath, Clare, D, Rich!

Dilys, who started me off on my RE journey, has much to do with me being able to write this today, and Tottie, whatever she's up to now, was in the past a superb encouragement and inspiration amongst a great deal of madness. Thank goodness for Jules!

Finally Jane's editing has been the key to getting the text in my head into its final – hopefully usable and valuable – format.

Lorraine Abbott

Exam advice, questions and hints revised and updated 2009 by Judith Anderson

The publishers would like to thank the following individuals, institutions and companies for permission to reproduce copyright illustrations in this book: **Cover** *tl* John Hulme, Eye Ubiquitous/Corbis, *tr* Corbis, *bl* © Reuters/Corbis, *br* © Sheldan Collins/Corbis. **pp.3**, 12, 13, 20, 24, 31, 45, 59 (*t*), 63 (*t*), 69, 83, 93, 101, 104 (*b*), 134 © Photos supplied by author; **pp.4**, 5 (*l*), 5 (*r*), 80 (*bl*), 104 (*t*) Rex Features; **p.26** RE:Quest, www.request.org.uk/Father Michael from Downside Abbey, www.downside.co.uk; **p.27** Sister Julie, http://anunslife.org; **p.33** (*tl*) Alexander Tsiaras/Science Photo Library; (*tr*) Edelmann/Science Photo Library; (*bl*) James Stevenson/Science Photo Library; (*br*) © Mediscan; **p.37** © 2005 Elizabeth Crews/TopFoto/ImageWorks; **p.40** © Karen Kasmauski/CORBIS; **p.41** © Reuters/CORBIS; **p.43** (*r*) HARRISE Emma Harris/PA Archive/PA Photos; **p.46** © Samaritans 2006, www.samaritans.org; **p.49** (*l*) © Jane Cooper/RSPCA; (*r*) Stuart Clarke/Rex Features; **p.59** (*b*) © Jim Loring/Tearfund – used by permission (www.tearfund.org); **p.60** (*t*) © Peter Turnley/CORBIS; (*m*) © David Cumming/Eye Ubiquitous/CORBIS; (*b*) © Ashley Cooper/CORBIS; **p.61** Bruno Vincent/Getty Images; **p.63** (*b*) REUTERS/Babu; **p.68** (*t*) Olycom SPA/Rex Features; (*b*) royalty-free image; **p.70** Christian Aid, www.christianaid.org.uk; **pp.71**, 102 BMS World Mission, www.bmsworldmission.org; **p.75** (*tl*) Kote Rodrigo/EFE/CORBIS; (*tr*) © Leif Skoogfors/CORBIS; **pp.75** (*m*), 91 (*tr*), 92 Sipa Press/Rex Features; **p.75** (*bl*) © Bob Sacha/Corbis; **p.80** (*tl*) Roger-Viollet/Rex Features; (*br*) REUTERS/Chris Helgren; **p.85** Alisdair Macdonald/Rex Features; **p.87** © Claudia Kunin/Corbis; **p.90** © 2004 Topham Picturepoint; **p.91** (*tl*) Everett Collection/Rex Features; (*bl*) Faithworks, www.faithworks.info; (*br*) Erik C Pendzich/Rex Features; **p.98** (*tl*) The Travel Library/Rex Features; (*m*) © Richard T. Nowitz/CORBIS; (*tr*) © Rudy Sulgan/Corbis; (*bl*) © Wilfried Krecichwost/zefa/Corbis; (*br*) © 2004 Tony Savino/TopFoto/ImageWorks; **p.103** Andrew Stuart/PA; **p.106** Peter Brooker/Rex Features; **p.107** (*t*), (*b*) © David Turnley/CORBIS; **p.109** Peter Macdiarmid/Getty Images; **p.110** © 2004 Mitch Wojnarowicz/TopFoto/ImageWorks; **p.111** Jens Hartmann/Rex Features; **p.114** (*tl*) Monsmart, www.monsmart.com; (*bl*) Design by Curtis R Doll Jr of Curtis Graphics/www.curtisgraphics.com/stgls; **p.114** (*r*) Hinz/Edith Nedrud; **p.118** (*l*) © Glyn Thomas/Alamy; (*m*) © Paul Salmon/Alamy; (*tr*) © Tony Cordoza/Alamy; (*br*) © Icon Digital Featurepix/Alamy; **p.122** Cartoon © Steve Bell 2008 All Rights Reserved; **p.123** (*l*) Noah Berger/AP/PA Photos; (*m*) Anwar Hussein/Getty Images; (*r*) Vincenzo Pinto/AFP/Getty Images; **p.124** (*r*) Tim Boyle/Getty Images; **p.127** By Mike Coles, from The Bible in Cockney, published by BRF, www.brf.org.uk, 2001, used by permission; **p.131** © Avalon/Handout/Reuters/Corbis; **p.132** (*t*) © STEPHEN HIRD/Reuters/Corbis.
The Publishers would also like to thank the following for permission to reproduce material in this book: **p.33** Ekklesia, www.ekklesia.co.uk; **p.39** 'Clinics prepare for "lifestyle" fertility treatment', by Ian Sample, *The Guardian*, 6 January 2006, Copyright Guardian News & Media Ltd 2006; **p.47** 'Animal rights activists target chain of children's nurseries linked to lab' by Owen Bowcott and Martin Wainwright, *The Guardian*, 29 September 2005, Copyright Guardian News & Media Ltd 2005; **p.58** One World Week, www.oneworldweek.org; **p.59** 'A long-haul plight', by Abigail Frymann, *Tear Times*, © Tearfund 2005; **p.64** London City Mission, www.lcm.org.uk; **p.104** 'He was murdered for no other reason than the colour of his skin', by Helen Carter, *The Guardian*, 29 September 2005, Copyright Guardian News & Media Ltd 2005; **p.121** (*t*) 'Religious Programmes – God-slots embrace the spirit of the age', by Sally Turner, *The Independent*, 22 May 2006, © The Independent; (*b*) 'ITV accused of 'abandoning religious TV' ', by Maggie Brown, *The Guardian*, 22 May 2008, Copyright Guardian News & Media Ltd 2008; **p.129** Damaris Trust, www.damaris.org.
The publishers would like to acknowledge use of the following extracts: **p.26** RE:Quest, www.request.org.uk/Father Michael from Downside Abbey, www.downside.co.uk; **p.27** Sister Julie, http://anunslife.org; **p.43** 'Mercy Killing', *The Daily Mail*, 8 December 2004; **p.50** National Anti-Vivisection Society (NAVS)/www.navs.org; **p.57** *'Telling the Story – Being Positive about HIV/AIDS'*, by the Missions and Public Affairs Council of the Church of England; **p.105** Church of England, www.cofe.anglican.org; **p.113** Press Association; **p.119** (*l*) Islam For Today, www.islamfortoday.com; **p.119** (*r*) Christian Broadcasting Network, www.cbn.com; **p.125** Simon Dillon/http://uk.god.tv. All Bible quotations are taken from the New International Version (NIV), published by Hodder Religious.

Every effort has been made to trace all copyright holders, but if any have been inadvertently overlooked the Publishers will be pleased to make the necessary arrangements at the first opportunity.

Although every effort has been made to ensure that website addresses are correct at time of going to press, Hodder Education cannot be held responsible for the content of any website mentioned in this book. It is sometimes possible to find a relocated web page by typing in the address of the home page for a website in the URL window of your browser.

Hachette UK's policy is to use papers that are natural, renewable and recyclable products and made from wood grown in sustainable forests. The logging and manufacturing processes are expected to conform to the environmental regulations of the country of origin.

Orders: please contact Bookpoint Ltd, 130 Milton Park, Abingdon, Oxon OX14 4SB. Telephone: +44 (0)1235 827720. Fax: +44 (0)1235 400454. Lines are open 9.00–5.00, Monday to Saturday, with a 24-hour message answering service. Visit our website at www.hoddereducation.co.uk.

© Lorraine Abbott 2009
First published in 2009 by
Hodder Education,
An Hachette UK company
338 Euston Road
London NW1 3BH

Impression number   5
Year   2013 2012 2011

Illustrations by Clive Spong at Linden Artists and Oxford Designers and Illustrators
Typeset in Gill Sans Light 10.5pt and produced by Gray Publishing, Tunbridge Wells
Printed in Dubai

A catalogue record for this title is available from the British Library

ISBN 978 0 340 98412 3

Contents

Introduction

This book has been written specifically to support the ethics topics of the OCR Religious Studies B (Philosophy and Applied Ethics) GCSE course. The book is divided into the following six ethics topics and looks at them from a Christian perspective:

- Topic 1 Christianity and Human Relationships ⎤
- Topic 2 Christianity and Medical Ethics   ⎬ Unit B603
- Topic 3 Christianity, Poverty and Wealth   ⎦

- Topic 4 Christianity, Peace and Justice ⎤
- Topic 5 Christianity and Equality   ⎬ Unit B604
- Topic 6 Christianity and the Media   ⎦

Each topic starts by outlining the key concepts that you will need to learn about in order to answer examination questions successfully.

About the exam

Each Unit is worth 25 per cent of the total GCSE marks (unless you are doing the short course and then each Unit is worth 50 per cent of the marks). The exam paper for each Unit is one hour long and contains a question on each of the three different topic areas within it. You will need to choose and then answer two questions from the three. Each question is worth 24 marks, so in total there will be 48 marks on each paper/unit. Each question is divided into five parts – you will need to attempt all the parts: (a), (b), (c), (d) and (e).

The exam questions aim to assess your level of knowledge and understanding of the material as well as your capabilities to analyse and evaluate different beliefs and attitudes. In order to achieve maximum marks, it is useful for you to be aware of what is generally expected for each type of question.

Question a)
This part of the question is worth one mark and your answer should show your knowledge and understanding of a concept. So, for instance, you might be asked 'What is pacifism?' and your answer should show that you know what 'pacifism' means.

Question b)
This part of the question is worth two marks and asks for two ideas within a concept. So, for instance, you might be asked 'What are Christian attitudes to fertility treatment?' and you would need to respond to the trigger word 'attitudes' by showing that some Christians would think it was a good idea and explain why and also that other Christians would not agree to it and explain why.

Question c)
This part of the question is worth three marks and asks for three ideas within a concept. So, for instance, you might be asked 'What do Christians believe about the purposes of marriage?' and you would need to give three different ideas/reasons why Christians believe marriage to be important.

Question d)

This part of the question is worth six marks and asks you to describe and explain a belief or attitude, while analysing the reasons Christians respond in this way. So, for instance, you might be asked to explain Christian beliefs about giving money to charity. You would need to include relevant Christian teachings to support the ideas in your answer. Try to include biblical quotes, but you must make sure you explain what these mean in order to show the examiner that you have understood the teaching. For example, 'Love thy neighbour' means to 'treat other people as you would like to be treated yourself'. You will also need to use specific religious words in these answers when they are relevant. For example, when answering a question on medical ethics you may wish to refer to the phrase 'sanctity of life' which shows the belief that all life is created by God and so is special.

Question e)

This part of the question is worth 12 marks and asks you to show different points of view in response to the statement given. So, for instance, you might be given the statement 'Abortion is always wrong' and you would need to refer to a Christian point of view in your answer, showing that there are different Christian approaches to this statement and then give your own personal response. Try to make that response different, if you can, to the ones you have mentioned previously. It is very important that you do give your own point of view otherwise you will not achieve high marks. You will need to support the Christian ideas with reference to Christian teachings/ biblical quotes. Again, explain them in your own words to show your understanding.

Make sure you answer what the question is asking. Many candidates do not achieve the grade they hoped to get because they failed to do this. For instance, if the question is asking you to discuss Christian ideas on divorce, make sure you stay focused on divorce and do not get sidetracked into discussing the different ideas on re-marriage.

Trigger words

The exam questions may ask for you to respond to various trigger words:

Attitudes	Are the ways in which a Christian might interpret their beliefs. This trigger word means that there are different Christian approaches and you should try to show that there are different ways in which a Christian might respond.
Beliefs	What Christians believe in/their faith.
Describe	This word is asking you to give information about something. Try not to just make a list of ideas, but show that you have lots of knowledge about an idea.
Explain	This word is asking you to say why something happens so you should use the word 'because'.
Respond	This word is asking you to show how and why a Christian would act.
Teachings	These are quotes/sayings/rules from the Bible or Church authorities.

About the book

At the start of every topic there is a short section called Key Concepts, which outlines the main ideas that you will learn about in the topic.

TASK

The tasks help you to record information, to respond to Christian beliefs and to develop your written communication in preparation for the exam. The tasks are varied and challenging – you should find them stimulating.

To discuss

Ethical issues raise different ultimate questions. For many people there are no clear-cut answers to these, and for this reason it is important for you to spend time discussing them with others. This feature encourages you to do this. Developing an understanding of others' views will help you to answer part e) questions on the exam paper.

STRETCH WHAT YOU KNOW

It is always good to extend your learning by using a variety of resources, for example the internet, or by engaging in more challenging tasks. To support the extension of your learning there are a number of these 'stretching tasks' throughout the book.

EXAM FOCUS...

There are exam questions throughout the book to give you practice in answering different types of exam question.

...HINTS

This feature gives you guidance on what to include in your exam answers and how to structure them.

 **Bible bitz**

You don't have to learn lots of quotes for your exam, but in order to explain Christian attitudes and beliefs you need to know what they are based on. The Bible Bitz feature gives you some biblical teachings to support your knowledge and understanding. If you cannot remember the exact quote in the exam do not panic. You can put the teaching into your own words and the examiner will know what you are referring to. If you cannot remember where in the Bible the quote comes from, do not try to guess.

 **Link it up**

The ability to link beliefs to behaviour is a skill needed when answering some of the parts of the questions. You need to be able to say what a Christian might do and why. This feature gives you the opportunity to practise this skill.

The ethical issues that you are studying are relevant to our society today, so much so that you can hear about them in the news all the time. This feature helps you to consider these issues in relation to current events.

Lorraine

This feature contains real views from real people with a Christian faith, showing how beliefs and attitudes apply to individuals' lives today.

Christianity and Human Relationships

Key Concepts

In this topic you will learn about:

- Christian beliefs about sexual relationships and contraception
- Christian marriage ceremonies and how they reflect and emphasise Christian teaching
- Christian responses to civil partnerships
- Christian beliefs about divorce and remarriage
- The roles of men and women in a Christian family
- The roles of men and women in the Church family.

Christians believe that marriage is given by God to unite two people, and that sex is part of this relationship as an expression of love and as a means of reproduction. There is disagreement among Christians about civil partnerships. For Christians, marriage should ideally be a lifelong commitment. However, sometimes divorce breaks up this relationship. Although Christians believe that divorce is not desirable, some Christians recognise that it is sometimes necessary. Christians may also have different views about the roles of men and women within a Christian family and within the Church family.

In the media we constantly hear stories or see images related to human relationships, such as those shown below and opposite. The media and society as a whole recognise and accept many different types of relationships – such as marriage, co-habitation, same-sex relationships – as well as the end of these relationships, sometimes meaning divorce.

Fathers 4 Justice: divorced fathers fighting for their rights to see their children. Why do you think some men are driven to take this kind of action?

A newly wed couple as shown in brides' magazines.

The front cover of *Grazia*, a weekly women's glossy magazine.

TASKS

1 Look at the images on page 4 and above.

▨ For each image, make a list of words to describe how it relates to human relationships.

▨ Imagine – if you were an alien visiting Earth, what would you think British society's views on sexual relationships, marriage and divorce were? Use your list of words to imagine what you would think. Give reasons for your answer.

2 What do you think a Christian might think about each of the images? Would they describe any of the aspects of human relationships shown as unacceptable? Explain your answer.

Christian beliefs about sexual relationships and contraception

Bible bitz

God blessed them and said to them, 'Be fruitful and increase in number'.
Genesis 1: 28

Do you not know that your body is a temple of the Holy Spirit, who is in you...You are not your own; you were bought at a price. Therefore honour God with your body.
1 Corinthians 6: 19–20

Link it up

Using the Church teachings and the Bible quotes above, explain in what order Christians would place love, sex and marriage in a relationship.

To discuss

1 Explain to the people you are sitting with what order you think it is right for sex, love and marriage to happen in. Remember to say why you hold this view.

2 How does your view compare with the views of others in your class?

TASK

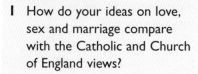

1 How do your ideas on love, sex and marriage compare with the Catholic and Church of England views?

Sexual relationships

Christians agree that one of the main roles of sex is to create new life and that it is a God-given expression of love between two people. For this reason, many Christians believe that a sexual relationship should be unique and exclusive to marriage. The Bible specifically links the act of sex with reproduction in Genesis 1: 28. For this reason, many Christians believe that sex should only occur between a man and a woman and that homosexual relationships are wrong.

However, in contemporary society some Christians accept that couples may live together and have sex as part of a committed relationship, even if they are not married. Similarly, some Christians also accept sexual relationships between a homosexual couple.

Nevertheless, all Christians would agree that casual sex is wrong, as the Bible teaches that FORNICATION is sinful.

The Catholic Church

The CATHOLIC CHURCH talks about sex as being the body's language. By this it means that sex is one way in which a married couple communicate their absolute, committed and exclusive love to one another.

The Catholic Church teaches that every time the act of sex occurs there should be the possibility for a new life to be created. This is because Catholics believe that God gave humans the gift of sex in order to reproduce and populate the Earth.

The Catholic Church accepts that homosexuals cannot change their sexual orientation. However, it teaches that sexual activity between homosexuals is a sin. This is because God gave humans sex as a means for procreation.

STRETCH WHAT YOU KNOW

In an address to Canada's new ambassador to the Holy See, Pope John Paul II noted that attempts to redefine marriage to include homosexual couples 'contradict right reason' and create 'a false understanding of the nature of marriage'.

What do you think John Paul II meant by 'false understanding of the nature of marriage'?

The Church of England

The CHURCH OF ENGLAND teaches that marriage is the proper place in which sexual relationships should occur, because sex is an act of love and loyalty reflecting total commitment, as expressed in the Christian wedding vows (see page 10). While it teaches that sex outside marriage falls short of God's purposes for human beings, the 1995 report *Something to Celebrate* recommended that Christians accept that COHABITATION including a sexual relationship is, for many people, a step towards commitment to marriage.

TASK

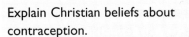

2 List the benefits and weaknesses of artificial and natural contraception.

EXAM FOCUS...

Explain Christian beliefs about contraception.

question d), 6 marks

...HINTS

▨ You would need to show that some Christians believe that contraception can be used and some do not think contraception should be used. You will need to explain why they have these beliefs.

▨ A biblical quote you could use to support your ideas could be: 'Go forth and multiply' (Genesis 1: 28).

▨ You could contrast the Catholic view about contraception to the different Protestant teachings.

▨ You could refer to the Christian idea about one of the purposes of marriage is to have children (procreation).

Contraception

CONTRACEPTION is sometimes known as 'birth control'. It can be divided into two broad types – artificial and natural.

▨ Artificial contraception

Artificial contraception is the use of a device, such as a condom, an operation such as a vasectomy, or a form of medication, such as the mini pill, to try to prevent an unwanted pregnancy.

▨ Natural contraception

Natural contraception is also aimed at reducing the chances of a woman becoming pregnant. This type of contraception includes a couple choosing to have sex during a woman's least fertile time in her menstrual cycle and the withdrawal method.

Sexually transmitted diseases

Some kinds of contraception, such as condoms, are not only used to reduce the likelihood of a woman getting pregnant, but also as a way of minimising the risk of sexually transmitted diseases. Contracting such diseases is more likely the more people a person has sex with.

Christian beliefs about contraception

The Catholic Church teaches that the use of artificial contraception is sinful. This is because it teaches that sex was God-given to humans for reproduction. It does, however, accept the use of some natural forms of contraception – this usually means only having sex at certain times during a woman's monthly cycle when she is at her least fertile. This allows a couple to regulate or space out the procreation of children. In reality, some Catholics disagree with the teaching of the Church about this and follow their conscience and use contraception.

In the past the Catholic Church has taught that condoms should never be used, even to help stop the spread of sexually transmitted diseases, and that ABSTINENCE should be used instead. Recently, however, one of the Church's Cardinals has accepted the use of condoms as the lesser of two evils in married couples where one had HIV/AIDS and could pass it on to the other, although the VATICAN has made no official comment on this.

Most other DENOMINATIONS teach that artificial contraception is acceptable. For example, the Church of England teaches that it is responsible to use contraception in order to ensure that children are planned and wanted.

Abstinence

There are campaigns and organisations that promote abstinence from sex until marriage. Their work is mainly directed at young people and reflects the beliefs of some Christians. One such organisation is Teen-Aid, which promotes the advantages of abstinence through poster campaigns, videos and training. Young people can indicate their commitment to sexual abstinence by filling in a commitment card like the one shown below. Other organisations that promote similar messages include Love Waits and The Silver Ring Thing. These organisations emphasise the Christian belief that sex was created by God as an expression of love within marriage, and that abstinence reflects a sense of self-worth and value.

Advantages of Abstinence

Freedom From
- pregnancy
- abortion
- pressures to marry before I am ready
- doubt, disappointment, worry, guilt or rejection
- sexually transmitted diseases
- trauma of relinquishing a baby
- exploitation by others
- bother or dangers of contraceptives

Freedom To
- be in control of my life
- develop self respect
- focus my energy on establishing and realizing life goals
- experience fuller communication in dating
- develop unselfish sensitivity
- enjoy being a teenager

Teen-Aid, Inc. • 723 E. Jackson • Spokane, WA 99207
1.800.357.2868 • www.teen-aid.org

Teen-Aid, Inc.©

Personal Commitment Card

I, _____
am a (virgin, secondary virgin). I have made a choice to remain abstinent until _____. I will be accountable to _____ for this decision.

Signed _____

Date _____   www.teen-aid.org

The front (A) and back (B) of Teen-Aid's commitment card

EXAM FOCUS...

Explain Christian attitudes
towards sex.

question d), 6 marks

TASKS

3 Read through the advantages of abstinence on the commitment card
on page 8. Do you agree with them? Explain your answer.

4 Design your own poster to promote the Christian belief in
abstinence until marriage. Use the artwork below to help you.

5 What is your view on organisations such as Teen-Aid promoting
abstinence?

...HINTS

■ You would need to respond to
the trigger word 'attitudes' and
show that there are different
Christian ideas about sex.

■ You might want to refer to the
way that some Christians believe
that sex should only be used
within marriage for 'unity' (one
flesh) to fulfil the marriage vow
'to love and to cherish'.

■ You might want to refer to the
fact that St Paul taught that the
body is a temple of the Holy
Spirit (1 Corinthians 6: 19) and
therefore Christians believe
casual sex is wrong.

■ You could show that some
Christians believe that sex
outside of marriage within a
loving committed relationship
is acceptable.

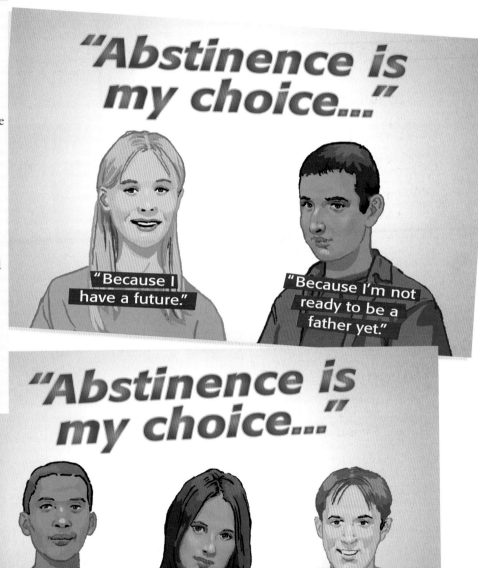

Christian marriage ceremonies

Description

Teaching

At the start of a Christian wedding ceremony, the minister explains the purpose of marriage. Usually this introduction will acknowledge that marriage is a gift from God, through which a man and a woman can grow together in love and trust. The minister will also explain that the couple will come together in sexual unity and that children may be born and looked after through the marriage union.

The minister then checks that there is no lawful reason why the couple may not be married.

This explanation of the purpose of marriage ensures that the couple and the witnesses understand the meaning of the ceremony. The service is not simply an act the couple make before family and friends, but also in front of God. This reminds the bride and groom of the lifelong, binding commitment that they are about to make to one another.

When someone is married to more than one person at a time it is known as bigamy. In the UK, this is illegal. Marriage relationships in the UK have to be monogamous. This means a person must only be married to one person at any one time. Christianity teaches that people should aim to have one monogamous relationship for life.

The couple exchange their vows in front of God and all the witnesses in the church. Wedding vows are promises to love and support one another in all circumstances until death.

from this day forward;
for better, for worse,
for richer, for poorer,
in sickness and in health,
to love and to cherish, (... and worship)
till death us do part;
according to God's holy law.
In the presence of God I make this vow.
    Anglican Book of Common Prayer, 2000

The vows, including those made during the exchange of the rings, break down the commitment that the couple are making to each other. They are important because they also can be referred back to during the course of a couple's married life. The vows provide:

- encouragement to stick to their original commitment to one another whatever situation they are in
- reassurance that their partner is committed to them, and has promised to be there for them until they die
- guidance on how to relate to their spouse – with love, respect and generosity.

The couple then exchange rings and the minister asks that God bless the vows they have made to one another. When the rings are exchanged the couple may make further promises to one another, for example:

[name], I give you this ring
as a sign of our marriage.
With my body I honour you,
all that I am I give to you,
and all that I have I share with you,
within the love of God,
Father, Son and Holy Spirit.

The rings are a symbol of the commitment that the couple have made to one another. They act as an outward sign to others that a person is married and unavailable for a sexual or marital relationship with anyone else.

Description		Teaching

Description

Prayers are said for the couple to ask for God's blessing on their marriage and their life together in all situations. The prayers often ask God to help the couple to be hospitable to others, to be faithful to God and that God will bless them with children to nurture. Hymns are usually sung during this part of the service.

Teaching

Through prayers the couple are encouraged to rely on God and to seek him for support during their married life together. God is involved in the relationship right from the very start. Christian couples believe that by keeping God at the centre of their lives and their marriage he strengthens their relationship with each other and guides them.

The hymns are often chosen to reflect the belief that love and marriage are from God, for example a hymn called *Love Divine*.

The couple sign the marriage register. Two witnesses also sign the document

The couple are then given their marriage certificate.

This is a civic, legal requirement in the UK.

To discuss

1 How can the vows made between the bride and groom be useful to them in their married life?

2 Can you think of examples of situations when a couple may need encouragement, reassurance or guidance?

To discuss

3 Mark says that he is committed to his wife for life. Do you think that this is a realistic promise?

4 Look back at the marriage ceremony on pages 10–11. What support would a Christian believe they have to help them to keep the promise of being committed to one person for life?

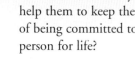

Bible bitz

The Lord God said, 'It is not good for the man to be alone. I will make a helper suitable for him.'
Genesis 2: 18

A man will leave his father and mother and be united to his wife, and the two will be become one flesh ... Therefore what God has joined together, let man not separate.
Mark 10: 7–9

Link it up

Look at the Bible quote from St Mark's Gospel above. What does the Bible mean when it talks about a man and a woman marrying and becoming 'one flesh'?

Mark

I got married at 22. Many of my friends thought this was too young to get married, and that I should be carefree and party. They felt that marriage at this age was taking on too much responsibility. I knew it was right to marry Clare. We had been seeing each other for over two years. As we are both committed Christians, we knew that marriage would be the next step in our relationship.

We both believe that sex is the most intimate that you can get with anyone, and it should be saved for and enjoyed in a married relationship. That doesn't mean it was easy, but waiting until we were married was an act of love to each other and to God.

We chose to marry in church; our promises in the wedding were to one another and to God. I was happy and proud to declare my love for Clare in front of all our friends and family.

Love in our marriage is not just the passionate and romantic feeling you get when you first fancy someone – it is about considering the other person's needs as well as your own. At times this is hard.

Even though I am sure there will be challenging situations in our marriage, I am committed to Clare for life. My wedding vows help me to focus on the promises I have made to Clare. A successful marriage is based on not taking the other person for granted – it is a relationship in which husband and wife learn to develop and mature in their love for each other throughout their lives together.

Most Churches offer support or classes before a couple marry. This is to help them understand fully the commitment that they are making and explore any potential disagreements they may have before they actually marry. How one VICAR supports couples is outlined below.

Rev. Jonathan Willans

As a vicar in the Church of England, I spend a lot of my time preparing couples for marriage, as well as helping already married couples who may be facing difficult times.

Every couple planning to get married is encouraged to attend the marriage preparation course run by the church. It provides useful advice on a wide range of issues, such as the importance of mutual trust, spending time together, sorting finances, resolving disagreements, coping with the in-laws, sex, parenting, etc.

The course is run over several evenings, the number of sessions depending on the time made available by the couple. At least three couples attend any one session. Evenings consist of watching a DVD on a particular topic and then discussing it over a glass of wine. Couples who attend say they find the course of real benefit.

Married couples often turn to the clergy if they are experiencing difficulty in their marriage. This is a common pastoral situation, which works almost as a 'counselling service'. Everything said and done is strictly confidential.

EXAM FOCUS...

Explain how a Christian marriage ceremony might guide a couple in their married life.

question d), 6 marks

...HINTS

- The question is asking you to think about the vows, which are considered to be rules for a marriage. So you would need to state a vow (or condition) such as to love and support their partner no matter what 'for better or worse' and then explain how this vow/rule might be useful in married life.
- You may wish to link the vow 'forsaking all others' to the seventh commandment: 'Do not commit adultery'.
- You may wish to comment on the fact that marriage is seen as a sacrament and therefore God has blessed the marriage, so the couple would want to make sure that the marriage did not fail.
- You could mention the purposes of marriage, which are outlined at the beginning of the service by the priest/vicar.

TASK

For Christians, marriage is all about LOVE. Marriage is:

L ifelong commitment

O bedience to God

V ows to one another

E xtending the family.

- Copy out the LOVE acrostic above.
- Use each of the four sentences as side headings. Write a paragraph under each one explaining how each is important in a Christian marriage.

Christian responses to civil partnerships

TASK

Read the information on civil partnerships. Imagine you are writing to your local MP on the issue of civil partnerships:
a) Write a letter from a Christian who is against same-sex partnerships.
b) Write a letter from a Christian who is for same-sex partnerships.
Make sure that in both responses you give clear reasons for the viewpoint that you are expressing.

> The fact of the matter is that God does not endorse this [a civil partnership] shall never endorse this and we are standing for the word of God and for the protection of our children.
>
> *The Reverend Doctor Ian Brown, the Free Presbyterian Church*

To discuss

1 Read the quote above. What do you think Reverend Brown meant when he said that by opposing same sex marriages he was standing for 'the protection of our children'?

2 Do you think civil partnerships are a necessary part of society today?

On 21 December 2005 it became legal in the UK for same-sex couples to recognise their union legally through civil partnerships, which give them the same rights in law as married couples. Couples who want to form a civil partnership have to register their intention with local authorities. Unlike a marriage the signing of the legal documents does not need to happen in public, but the couple may choose to have a ceremony if they want. The partnership can be registered in a register office or in any approved premises and the couple receive a certificate of their partnership. By law in the UK a marriage has to happen between 'one man' and 'one woman' a civil partnership is therefore not a marriage. Christians have different responses to civil partnerships.

Christian responses

The Catholic Church and the Church of England

The Catholic Church and the Church of England are against civil partnerships and do not perform them. This is because of their teachings about sexual relationships (see page 6). Both Churches teach marriage is the proper place in which sexual relationships should occur with the main role of sex being to create new life. Therefore, performing a civil partnership would suggest that homosexual sex is as acceptable as married heterosexual sex which is against their teaching. They also think that making civil partnerships the same as heterosexual marriages in the eyes of the Church would undermine their teaching that it is best that children be raised by their biological mother and father.

The clergy of The Church of England have been told by the House of Bishops not to carry out services of blessings of civil partnerships. However, in June 2008 the Reverend Martin Dudley carried out a blessing ceremony after the civil partnership of Reverend Peter Cowell and the Reverend Dr David Lord. Other homosexual clergy in the Church of England believe that civil partnerships should be recognised and blessed by the Church. The Reverend Paul Collier, an openly homosexual Church of England vicar, believes that by not doing so the Church is 'failing to respond to an opportunity to celebrate and affirm love, fidelity and commitment'.

Other Christian responses

There are some Christians who believe that civil partnerships should be acceptable to the Church. They believe that civil partnerships provide companionship, unity and stability in the same way that heterosexual marriage does. Christians who believe this think that civil partnerships reflect the biblical value of EQUALITY and God's desire to bless faithful lifelong marriages regardless of the sex of the couple. At the 1996 Unitarian Universalist General Assembly, delegates voted overwhelmingly that because of 'the inherent worth and DIGNITY of every person', same-sex couples should have the same freedom to marry that other couples have.

Link it up

1 Using the Church teachings and the Bible quotes opposite, explain why many Christians oppose civil partnerships.
2 How do some Christians support the view that homosexual civil partnerships are acceptable?

BB Bible bitz

But for Adam no suitable helper was found. So the Lord God caused the man to fall into a deep sleep; and while he was sleeping, he took one of the man's ribs and closed up the place with flesh. Then the Lord God made a woman from the rib he had taken out of the man, and he brought her to the man.

The man said,

'This is now bone of my bones
and flesh of my flesh;
she shall be called "woman,"
for she was taken out of man.'

For this reason a man will leave his father and mother and be united to his wife, and they will become one flesh.

Genesis 2: 20–24

If a man lies with a man as one lies with a woman, both of them have done what is detestable.

Leviticus 20: 13

Do you not know that the wicked will not inherit the kingdom of God? Do not be deceived: Neither the sexually immoral nor idolaters nor adulterers nor male prostitutes nor homosexual offenders nor thieves nor the greedy nor drunkards nor slanderers nor swindlers will inherit the kingdom of God.

1 Corinthians 6: 8–10

EXAM FOCUS...

'God would never approve of civil partnerships.'
Discuss this statement. You should include different, supported points of view and a personal viewpoint. You must refer to Christianity in your answer.

question e), 12 marks

HINTS

- Remember – it is important to show different points of view and also your own personal point of view.

- This question is asking you to discuss and evaluate (look at the arguments for and against) and then come to a conclusion on whether the statement is true or false. You may not want to agree or disagree entirely – that is fine but you must support your conclusion with a valid reason.

- You could agree with the statement by referring to the fact that some Christians would rely on biblical references such as God made male and female to be 'one flesh' (Genesis 2: 24) or other quotes to support their view that same-sex relationships are wrong. Note: if you cannot remember where in the Bible a quote comes from do not make it up.

- You could disagree with the statement by showing that some Christians may state that because Jesus showed compassion, everyone should be treated equally: 'Love thy neighbour'. Therefore civil partnerships are a good idea.

- Then give your own personal view.

Christian beliefs about divorce and remarriage

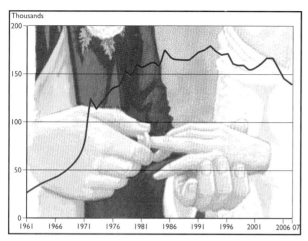

The number of divorces in the UK per year, 1961–2007

In 2004, the number of divorces granted in the UK increased to 167,116 from 166,737 in 2003. This was the highest number of divorces since 1996, and the fourth successive annual increase. However, since then divorce rates have fallen – there were 144,220 divorces in 2007. Below are several different views about divorce.

To discuss

1 What do the statistics in the graph show you about divorce rates over the past four decades?

2 What do you think are some of the reasons for divorce?

Divorce is necessary in our society, because marriages don't always work out. Sometimes people think they'll be able to get along but then discover that they disagree on so many things that it is better for them to split up.

Sometimes divorce is used as a quick fix – instead of working at a relationship and getting help for their problems, people just get divorced. I don't think this is right. Marriage needs to be worked at.

When a person is being abused in any way in a relationship, then I think divorce is right. No one has a right to hurt someone else.

Divorce is wrong if a couple have children. They should stay together for their sake.

If a married person has an affair then I think divorce is OK. After all, the trust in the relationship has already been broken.

If people have promised to stay together for life then that is what they should do.

TASK

1 ▦ Divide your page into two columns as shown below.

Views for divorce	Views against divorce

▦ Read the different views about divorce.

▦ Identify the reason that each 'talking head' gives for or against divorce and record it in the correct column in your table.

▦ Add any other reasons for and against divorce that you can think of. Leave space to add any more views after you've read about the Christian views on page 18.

▦ Explain which views on divorce you agree with.

When marriages do get into difficulty, churches usually offer some kind of support or counselling (an example of which is described by Reverend Willans on page 13), or they may refer a couple on to a specific relationship counselling service. An example of such a service is Relate.

Case Study: *Relate*

Relate is the largest relationship counselling service in the UK. One of the major parts of its work is to help couples understand what is happening in their relationship and to change it for the better. Relate offers support to individuals, couples and families. It does this through counselling, workshops, mediation and face-to-face meetings. In 2008, 73 per cent of people who had gone through relationship counselling with Relate said that their relationship had improved.

Relate also works in communities in four main ways:

- School work – providing relationship courses and developing peer listening schemes with the aim of helping young people to develop positive relationships with others.

- Prison work – establishing programmes to help prisoners to develop and sustain relationships with their families.
- Tackling relationship problems – one of the major causes of homelessness is relationship breakdown. Relate works with local authorities to tackle relationship problems within families that may lead to homelessness.
- Supporting professionals and volunteers – Relate provides courses and workshops for people who work within communities in order to develop their communication skills as well as their ability to deal with relationship issues.

(From the Relate website – www.relate.org.uk)

S T R E T C H WHAT YOU KNOW

Using the 'About us' link on Relate's website (www.relate.org.uk), find out the following information:

1 Who are the peer listening schemes for and what are their objectives?

2 When did Relate start its work with prisons and how does it support prisoners and their families?

3 What service does Relate offer to local authorities in targeting homelessness?

Hey, presto, one flesh becomes two!

TASKS

2　Why do people find the idea of a magician actually sawing a person in two so unbelievable?

3　Can you make a link between the cartoon and what you think a Christian attitude to divorce might be? Consider the Bible quote that teaches that in marriage two people become 'one flesh' (Mark 10: 7–9) to help you.

Christian teachings

Christians believe that a marriage relationship is entered into as a lifelong commitment. However, Christians have different attitudes to the subject of divorce.

The Catholic Church

The Catholic Church is aware of the increasing rate of divorce and knows that many people believe that it is often the best option when a relationship has broken down. However, it believes that marriage is indissoluble. Catholics believe that it cannot be broken by humans, as the wedding vows are made to God as well as to each other. For this reason, they do not accept divorce. The Catholic Church teaches that divorce is simply breaking the legal agreement made in marriage, not the holy agreement made with God. So divorce is considered sinful.

When Catholic couples divorce they are encouraged not to take part in the EUCHARIST and remarriage is considered an ADULTEROUS ACT (ADULTERY). Divorce is not believed to be recognised by God. However, the Church understands that divorce is painful. Catholics believe support should be given to anyone who has gone through divorce, even though they do not agree with it.

When a couple are experiencing difficulties in their marriage, the Catholic Church teaches that they may separate but that they should work on trying to restore their marriage and not enter into any other sexual relationships.

The Catholic Church does, however, annul marriages. This means agreeing that the promises made in marriage were void and that the marriage is discounted. One reason for an annulment would be if either person had been forced into the marriage. Once a marriage has been annulled, individuals are free to marry someone else.

The Church of England

The Church of England believes that couples should work hard to keep their vow of a lifelong commitment to each other. It does, however, recognise that sometimes it may be impossible for a couple to remain together, for example when there is abuse or adultery in the marriage.

If divorce does occur, the Church of England sees it as a priority to care for the couple. If a divorcee wants to remarry in church then it is up to the vicar whether or not to consent. The vicar will take into consideration why the person got divorced in the first place and what efforts were made to keep the first marriage together. If, for example, the person wishing to remarry in a church divorced as a result of their spouse's adultery then it is likely that the vicar would agree to the new marriage taking place in church.

The Church of England believes it has a responsibility to protect the understanding of marriage as a lifelong commitment, and so any remarriage in a church would only happen after careful consideration. In its document *Marriage* the Church says that 'a further marriage after a divorce is an exceptional act; that it must be approached with great honesty; and that the Church itself has a part in deciding whether or not a marriage in such circumstances should take place in the context of church worship.'

To discuss

3 Identify what is happening in each of the illustrations. Do you think the Church of England would find divorce an acceptable option in any of the situations that you have identified?

4 What do you think the two quotes (A and B) mean? Bear in mind that Zsa Zsa Gabor married nine times.

5 Discuss whether you think either of the quotes reflects Church teachings on divorce.

BB Bible bitz

It has been said, 'Anyone who divorces his wife must give her a certificate of divorce.' But I tell you that anyone who divorces his wife, except for marital unfaithfulness, causes her to become an adulteress, and anyone who marries the divorced woman commits adultery.

Matthew 5: 31–32

The two will become one flesh. So they are no longer two, but one. Therefore what God has joined together, let man not separate.

Mark 10: 8–9

A wife must not separate from her husband. But if she does, she must remain unmarried or else be reconciled to her husband. And a husband must not divorce his wife.

1 Corinthians 7: 10–11

Hazel

When a marriage breaks up, the ripples spread far and wide. Divorce is not a private matter between two individuals. It involves everyone in the family, friends, colleagues at work and, above all, any children.

In my work as a teacher I often meet children struggling to keep up a good relationship with both their parents who are divorced, or who have to live with one parent when they need and love both.

Marriage is meant to be a lifelong commitment to one person. It is life-enhancing, brings a unique sense of fulfilment and an opportunity to mature as an individual. This ideal is, sadly, not always achieved. The relationship can become destructive, bringing misery to all.

Jesus himself recognised the existence of divorce, but he did not condone remarriage.

The Catholic Church, to which I belong, teaches that when two people are no longer able to live together they may separate but not divorce, because marriage is for life. Catholics may therefore not marry again while their partner lives. I sometimes think this teaching is very harsh, but I also believe it is a way of demonstrating how very seriously marriage is regarded.

Link it up

Which Bible quotes can be linked to which of the Church teachings? Use two columns to help you write down your answer. In one column, list the different Church teachings (see page 18) and in the other list the Bible quotes. Then draw lines from one to the other to show where the links are.

TASK

4 Add Christian views for and against divorce to the table you produced in Task 1, page 17. Use the Church teachings on page 18, the Bible quotes on this page and Hazel's views to help you to do this.

the problem page

Dear Sarah,

I really don't know who to talk to. I feel I am trapped and unable to do anything about it. I married my husband Paul five years ago when I was just 20. Paul is a genuinely loving man but this is part of the problem. I feel smothered. Whatever I do, wherever I go, he wants to know all about it, or he comes out with me. He says he just can't bear being apart from me. I need space and time to be myself and to do my own thing. I have tried to explain this to him but he just gets all defensive and makes stupid suggestions about me having secret affairs. What should I do?

From Ann

- -

Dear Ann

You must take control over your life and your relationship. Paul is manipulating you, using your love for him to stop you living your life. If he loved you, he would trust you. If you want your relationship with this man to work you must sit down together and explain how you feel and what needs to change. If he won't listen, I suggest you get yourself out of the relationship and move on with your life. You say he won't listen and that he suggests that you are being unfaithful – clearly he is insecure and not as certain of your love as you are of his. Marriage is a two-way commitment of love and trust. If that commitment isn't there from both of you, then perhaps the marriage is already over.

TASKS

5 Select and write down any of the advice that Sarah gives that a Christian would not agree with.

6 Write a response to the problem page letter from a Christian viewpoint explaining what Ann should do in her situation.

EXAM FOCUS...

Describe Christian beliefs about divorce.

question d), 6 marks

...HINTS

- This question is asking you to show what you know about Christian teachings towards divorce. You can use the teachings from the Bible or from the different denominations (Churches).
- You could include what the Catholics believe about divorce and their teachings on annulment.
- You could refer to the teachings of Jesus, such as '... let man not separate' (Mark 10: 9) or teachings from the Old Testament.
- To help you, look at the teachings on page 18.

The roles of men and women in a Christian family

Christianity believes a woman's central role in the family is as a wife and a mother …

… that the man is the main wage earner …

… and that he is the leader of the family.

However, women and men's roles are of equal value.

To discuss

1 Do you think there are any jobs or roles in family life that are more suitable to either men or women? Use the images above as a starting point for your discussion.

Christian teachings

Christianity teaches about the belief in the equality of all people. This includes equality between men and women. Christians tend to have differing views of the roles of men and women within the family, but all agree that, whatever role a person takes, they are valuable to God.

Pope John Paul II spoke of men and women having equal dignity and responsibility in the family as well as in society. In his exhortation *Familiaris Consortio*, he said: 'In creating the human race "male and female", God gives man and woman an equal personal dignity with the rights and responsibilities proper to the human person.'

The Catholic Church recognises the equal right of opportunity for women to work outside the home alongside men. However, it values the role of the woman in the home as highly as any career she may choose to have. The Catholic Church, alongside many other Christians, believes that a woman should not feel under social pressure to have a career if she would rather be a full-time housewife and mother. For example, John Paul II also said that 'men should truly esteem and love women with total respect for

Wives, submit to your husbands as to the Lord. For the husband is the head of the wife as Christ is the head of the church ... Now as the church submits to Christ, so also wives should submit to their husbands in everything.

Ephesians 5: 22–24

There is neither Jew nor Greek, slave nor free, male nor female, for you are all one in Christ Jesus.

Galatians 3: 28

The LORD God said, 'It is not good for the man to be alone. I will make a helper suitable for him.'

Genesis 2: 18

Wives, in the same way be submissive to your husbands ... Husbands, in the same way be considerate as you live with your wives, and treat them with respect as the weaker partner.

I Peter 3: 1–7

their personal dignity, and society should create and develop conditions favouring work in the home.'

Many Christians believe a man should be as involved in family life as a woman. These beliefs focus on the equality of all people and on the mutual needs of a couple for one another. St Ambrose wrote of husbands: 'You are not her master but her husband; she was not given to you to be your slave, but your wife ... Return her attentiveness to you and be grateful to her for her love.'

Some Christians interpret teachings in the Bible to mean that women are literally men's helpers, and that men are the leaders in a marriage relationship. For this reason, some women still choose to vow obedience to their husband during their wedding ceremony. Moreover, some Christians consider women to be weaker than men because in the story of Adam and Eve in Genesis, the woman, Eve, gave into temptation before the man, Adam.

Christians who hold these more traditional views see women's role as primarily being in the home caring for the children. They see the man's role as the main wage earner and provider for his family. The role of the woman in the home has equal value to the work of the man, but each role is unique to the person's gender.

The role a man or woman takes within a Christian family will depend on their own understanding of the Bible teachings.

TASKS

1 Divide your page into three columns, like the example below.
2 In the left-hand column, write down in bullet points each of the different Christian beliefs about the roles of men and women.
3 In the middle column match each of the pictures on page 22 with the beliefs. Use the picture captions to do this.
4 Now read the Bible quotes on this page, and in the right-hand column match the Bible quotes up with the Christian beliefs and the pictures.
5 Some quotes and captions may be used more than once.

Christian beliefs	Picture caption	Bible quote
Men and women are equal value to God.	Role equality	There is neither Jew of nor Greek, slave nor free, male nor female, for you are all one in Christ Jesus.

STRETCH WHAT YOU KNOW

1 Explain what you think the Catholic Church means when it refers to both sexes being 'an image of the power and tenderness of God'.

2 Explain how, in a marriage relationship, one can observe the equal dignity of men and women in different ways.

To discuss

2 What dilemma does Emma say she and her husband have?

3 What may affect a couple's decisions about the roles that they have within their family?

4 Do you think that the traditional Christian beliefs about the role of men and women in the family are practical today?

Emma

People always seem to get worked up about the role of men and women in a marriage relationship. I've been married for seven years and when I made my vows to my husband I promised to obey him. Peter promised to love me. After the wedding some of my friends joked that I'd have to jump to Peter's every order! You know the sort of thing: cooking, washing and so on. But to us it was so different to that idea. As a Christian Peter believes that as head of our family he has to work towards the kind of love Christ has for us. This type of love is completely sacrificial; it's not a demanding and selfish love. So if Peter really does keep his promise to love me, he won't make any unfair or completely selfish demands on me. His love will put me first.

We both work at the moment. We need both our incomes to pay for our mortgage. I like working; it helps me to feel challenged and stimulated. I couldn't stay at home all the time. However, if we ever had children I believe it would be right for one of us to stay at home. God has given parents the huge responsibility of bringing up children. My only worry is whether we could actually afford to do this. For us this is a real dilemma.

EXAM FOCUS...

'Women should always obey their husbands.'
Discuss this statement. You should include different, supported points of view and a personal viewpoint. You must refer to Christianity in your answer.

question e), 12 marks

...HINTS

- Remember – it is important to show different points of view and also your own personal point of view.
- This question is asking you to discuss and evaluate (look at the arguments for and against) and then come to a conclusion on whether the statement is true or false. You may not want to agree or disagree entirely – that is fine but you must support your conclusion with a valid reason.
- Reference could be made to Paul's command for wives to submit to their husbands (Ephesians 5: 22) and the fact that traditionally, in the marriage ceremony, women did promise to obey their husbands.
- You may wish to refer to the Genesis creation stories in which Genesis 1 shows men and women to be equal made in the image of God (Genesis 1: 27) whereas in Genesis 2, Eve is made to be a helper to Adam (Genesis 2: 18).
- You may wish to refer to the fact that some Christians see women as the weaker sex because they were the first to sin (Genesis 3: 6).
- Remember to include your own personal view on the question.

The role of men and women in the Church family

EXAM FOCUS...

Explain Christian beliefs on the role of men and women in the Church family.

question d), 6 marks

...HINTS

- This question is asking you to show why there are different Christian ideas on what men and women can do within the Church. You will need to support these ideas with reference to Biblical and Church teachings.
- You may wish to show that some men and women want to devote their lives entirely to God and spend their time in worship instead of becoming married and raising a family. You could use Mother Teresa as an example of someone called by God to devote her life to caring for the poor because by helping them she was helping Jesus (parable of the Sheep and the Goats).
- You could refer to the fact that the Catholic Church is still against women becoming priests because of the teachings of Paul in the New Testament. The second chapter of Genesis also supports this idea.
- You could refer to the fact that women play different roles in the Church, for instance being an active member of the Mothers' Union or even helping to decorate the church with flowers.

In the Catholic Church only men may become priests and bishops. The Pope is therefore always male. Catholic priests and bishops have to remain CELIBATE – in a sense they are married to Christ and his work in the Church.

However, women do have an important role in the Church and can take an active part by becoming extraordinary ministers of the Holy Communion (giving out the consecrated bread and wine at MASS) or visiting the sick and those in need.

In the Church of England both men and women can become vicars, however bishops and the leader of the Church, the Archbishop, is always a man. Within the Church there is disagreement over this division, with many ANGLICANS believing that if a woman can be ORDAINED as a vicar then they should also be allowed to become bishops. Others maintain that the greater level of authority and oversight held by a bishop should remain the role of men only.

In both the Catholic Church and the Church of England the priest or vicar spends time preparing for and celebrating the SACRAMENTS. Each day some time is set aside for personal, private prayer. A priest or vicar will also visit the sick, visit people in their homes and work with the various organisations in the PARISH. The priest or vicar is a spiritual leader in the community, making himself or herself available to the needs of the people in the parish.

STRETCH WHAT YOU KNOW

The Mothers' Union is a Christian Organisation that has over 3.6 million members worldwide. Its mission is:

- to promote and support married life
- to encourage parents in their role to develop the faith of their children
- to maintain a worldwide fellowship of Christians united in prayer, worship and service
- to promote conditions in society favourable to stable family life and the protection of children
- to help those whose family life has met with adversity.

They operate many projects around the world. For example, in Burundi the Mothers' Union is involved in supporting refugees and caring for orphans. It has also started income generating projects based on agriculture, breeding animals, handicraft and bee keeping.

1 Go to www.themothersunion.org and follow links from 'What we do' to the project work. As examples of the role of women in the international church family find out what the Mothers' Union is doing in York, Australia and Congo.
2 How does the existence of the Mothers' Union give opportunities for women to be involved in the Church family?
3 To what extent do you think the work of the Mothers' Union is relevant to society today?

TASKS

Read the day in the life of a monk and answer the following questions.

1 What is the structure of a monk's day based around?
2 Why do you think there are significant times of silence built into a monk's day?
3 What reasons can you think of that may lead a man or woman to monastic life?

Monks and nuns

Some Christians believe they have been called by God to become a nun or a monk. These are people who take special vows committing themselves to a religious life. This may involve leaving mainstream society and living a life of prayer and contemplation in a monastery or convent.

A day in the life of a monk at Downside Abbey in Somerset

(Used with kind permission of RE:Quest, www.request.org.uk, and Father Michael from Downside Abbey, www.downside.co.uk)

7.30 am   Breakfast, taken in silence.

8.35 am   Mass. The whole community is gathered together for the celebration of the eucharist.

9.15 am   After Mass, the monks go about their different jobs, whether it be teaching in the school, looking after a local parish, or dealing with visitors.

1.10 pm   Midday prayer. In the middle of our working day, we pause to remember that it is God who gives value to our work and sustains us in our labours. This is followed by lunch. We begin by singing grace together; then, as we eat in silence, one of the brethren reads to us an extract which the Abbot has chosen: it might be an academic article from a journal, or a sermon or lecture.

5.45 pm   Vespers. Vespers is one of the 'hinges' of the day. For most of the community, the working day is done, and it is time to give thanks to God for the graces he has given during the day, in prayer and singing. After Vespers, there is another half-hour of silence so that we can pray privately or meditate on a passage of the Bible.

6.45 pm   Supper. As with the other meals, this is taken in silence, but the reading is lighter and more entertaining: it may be biography, history or travel writing.

7.15 pm   Community recreation. After we have tidied up in the refectory, this is the time to relax together as a monastic family, to swap news, ideas, stories, and just to be together.

8.00 pm   Compline. The last part of the Divine Office, which we sing by heart in the darkened church. After Compline there is silence in the monastery until breakfast the next morning.

Sister Julie

What motivates a person to become a nun?

You asked what my motivation was for becoming a nun. Well, I didn't really plan on becoming a nun. My motivation was to live my life the best way I could as a young, single, Catholic woman. I knew my options were single life, married life and religious life. I figured that I was destined for married life. I always wanted to be married and to be a mum. But, I decided I'd check out the religious thing just to say 'been there, done that' ... so I wouldn't have any doubts about that not being my call. Well, that didn't happen. It turns out it was my call. I think deep down, I recognised that I was most fully myself when I was in tune with God. It just so happened that for me, that meant living the lifestyle of a religious. For others, it may mean living a married life, being a parent, becoming ordained or choosing single life. Whatever lifestyle God calls us to is it, the best one for us. I realised that to be true to myself meant that I had to let go of something and let God do the driving. I still am quite a back-seat driver, but more and more I am able to say 'not my will, Lord, but yours be done'.

Being a nun is more of a way of life than it is a career. I think of a career as something that at the end of the day or week, I can come home and do my ordinary stuff. I'm 'off duty' so to speak. Just like being married is not a career, being a nun is not really a career because being a nun is part of who I am. As with married life, our vows are for life — in good times and in bad.

In a way, I wasn't the one who first chose this life of being a nun. It's like it chose me. I know that sounds kind of weird, but it's true. It's not something I ever would have thought would 'fit' me. Yet, by golly, it does. Once I realised that this is what God was calling me to, I had to take the time and space to choose it for myself, to make God's call my own, to embrace it freely. After some major resisting, running, and denial, I was able to freely choose this life, knowing that it is the best way I can be me and serve God and the world.

(Used with kind permission from Sister Julie. You can find Sister Julie's blog at http://anunslife.org)

To discuss

1 Before becoming a nun what were sister Julie's expectations for her life?

2 In what way does she say her life as a nun is like that of a mother?

3 What do you think sister Julie means when she says she is most fully herself when she is in tune with God?

LET'S REVISE

Christian marriage ceremonies

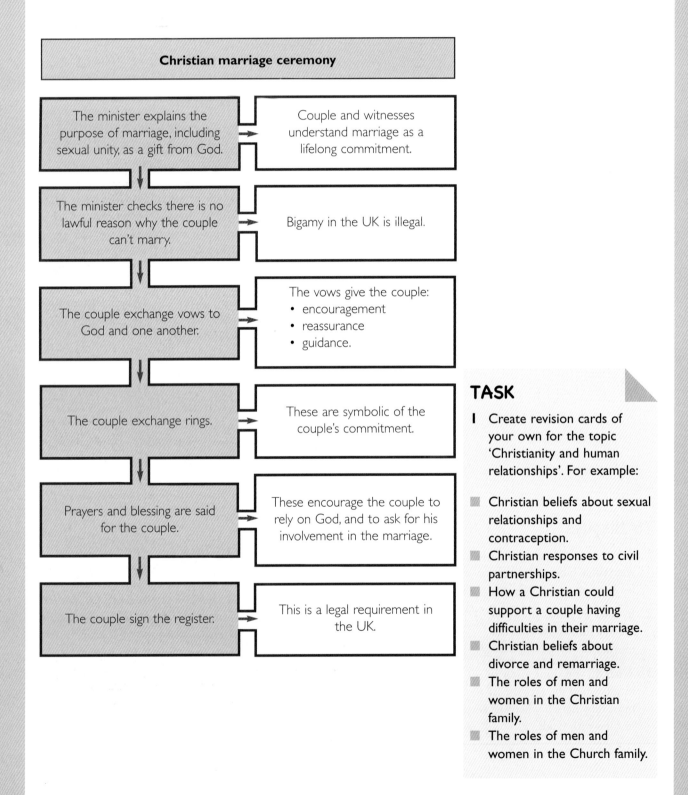

Christian marriage ceremony

The minister explains the purpose of marriage, including sexual unity, as a gift from God.	Couple and witnesses understand marriage as a lifelong commitment.
The minister checks there is no lawful reason why the couple can't marry.	Bigamy in the UK is illegal.
The couple exchange vows to God and one another.	The vows give the couple: • encouragement • reassurance • guidance.
The couple exchange rings.	These are symbolic of the couple's commitment.
Prayers and blessing are said for the couple.	These encourage the couple to rely on God, and to ask for his involvement in the marriage.
The couple sign the register.	This is a legal requirement in the UK.

TASK

1 Create revision cards of your own for the topic 'Christianity and human relationships'. For example:

- Christian beliefs about sexual relationships and contraception.
- Christian responses to civil partnerships.
- How a Christian could support a couple having difficulties in their marriage.
- Christian beliefs about divorce and remarriage.
- The roles of men and women in the Christian family.
- The roles of men and women in the Church family.

LET'S REVISE

a) What is meant by contraception? *1 mark*

■ You need to give a short explanation as to what contraception is – i.e. something that is used to prevent a baby from happening.

b) Describe Christian attitudes towards sex before marriage. *2 marks*

■ The keyword in this question is 'attitudes' – this word shows you that Christians have different ideas on whether or not sex should happen before a marriage. So give one idea that shows it is wrong and one idea that shows when it might be allowed to happen

c) Explain why Christians believe the wedding ceremony to be important. *3 marks*

■ You need to give three ideas. These could include the view that God witnesses the saying of the vows; that God intended man and woman to be married (one flesh); that Jesus performed his first miracle at a wedding showing that he blessed the union; that marriage is a sacrament, etc.

d) Explain the different roles of men and women within a Christian family. *6 marks*

■ You will need to show that some Christians have a traditional view where the men and women have different roles and link the idea to a biblical teaching. And also show that other Christians believe that men and women can have the same roles if they wish and link this to a biblical teaching.

e) 'Divorce is always wrong.'
Discuss this statement. You should include different, supported points of view and a personal viewpoint. You must refer to Christianity in your answer. *12 marks*

■ Remember – it is important to show different points of view and also your own personal point of view.
■ This question is asking you to discuss and evaluate (look at the arguments for and against) and then come to a conclusion on whether the statement is true or false. You may not want to agree or disagree entirely – that is fine, but you must support your conclusion with a valid reason.
■ You will need to show the different Christian views on divorce and link them to relevant biblical and Church teachings.
■ Remember to include your own personal viewpoint.

Christianity and Medical Ethics

Key Concepts

In this topic you will learn about:

- The SANCTITY OF LIFE
- Christian attitudes towards abortion
- Christian responses to issues raised by fertility treatment
- Christian responses to issues raised by cloning
- Christian attitudes towards euthanasia and suicide
- Christian beliefs about the use of animals in medical research.

The key concept that influences Christian thinking on medical issues is that life is holy as it is a gift from God. Another way to express this is to say that life is sacred – this idea is known as the sanctity of life. Christians will apply this idea differently to various ethical medical issues in order to decide what they believe is right.

TASK

Most valuable ———————————————————————————————— Valueless

1. ■ Draw a line like the one shown above.

   ■ Look at the list below. Place each person from the list somewhere on the line to illustrate their value according to you.

Doctor	Terminally ill person
Murderer	Foetus
Yourself	

   ■ Explain why you have put each person at that point on the line.

   ■ Discuss as a class the different ways people have completed this task. Why do you think there are differences in your views?

The sanctity of life

Christianity teaches that all human life is a precious gift from God. Another way of saying this is to call life sacred. Every person is of equal worth to God, although a person may do something which is better or worse than another person. It is also a Christian belief that a human's age, health or ability does not make the person more or less valuable; this is why the concept of the sanctity of life is so important in considering medical ethics.

The sanctity of life means that life should be treated with respect as an act of worship to God. Any mistreatment of the human body, for example through the use of illegal drugs, goes completely against this religious teaching and is unacceptable to believers. Christians believe that:

- each person should honour God through their bodies and in the way that they live their lives
- God not only gives life but he sustains it and guides people in each situation they are in, if they have faith in him.

The Christian teaching on the sanctity of life can be used in questions on the following topics:

- abortion
- euthanasia
- EMBRYO research and fertility treatment
- peace and justice.

To discuss

1. Where do you think a believer in the sanctity of life would place each person on the list from task 1? Give reasons to support your answer.

TASKS

2 Read Mark's account below. What behaviour do you think goes against the belief in the sanctity of life? Give reasons for your answer.

3 Explain whether you agree or disagree with Mark's view that treating life as sacred is beneficial to both individuals and society.

Mark

I am a committed Christian and my faith helps me to consider not only how to live my own life, but also how to value life itself. I try to think about others as God's creation, knowing that we are all here for a purpose. This helps me to treat people equally regardless of their race, religion or ability. I see what I do as part of my worship to God, so I avoid getting drunk or smoking. These things damage our bodies, and I believe this is abusing the gift of life that God has given to me.

I do think that if more people valued others the way they value themselves the world would be a better place. Think about it – most crime and bullying happens out of a belief by the perpetrator that other people and their feelings are not worth as much as they are. Other stuff that worries me includes just how quick it can be for a woman to get an abortion – I wonder whether the FOETUS has any value at all. Then there's the idea that helping someone to die using euthanasia might be OK. Surely that is like saying that some life is no longer worth living, that it is worthless. I think these attitudes lead to making some individuals feel worthless, whereas my view is all about giving respect and value to every individual. I think that is a far more positive approach to life.

To discuss

2 Read the quote below. Explain whether you think a Christian would agree with Sartre's view of life.

'Every existing thing is born without reason, prolongs itself out of weakness, and dies by chance.'

Jean-Paul Sartre, philosopher (1905–1980)

STRETCH WHAT YOU KNOW

Jean-Paul Sartre was a philosopher and an atheist. He did not believe that life was sacred. Research what he thought by going to www.answers.com and searching his name. Then write a paragraph explaining his view on human life.

Christian attitudes towards abortion

Christian teachings

Christian teaching on abortion is not simple. Generally Christians' belief in the sanctity of life means they have concerns about abortion, but their attitudes towards it differ.

No Christian Church believes that abortion should be encouraged, and most agree that it should only be used in the most serious circumstances.

The Catholic Church

The CATHOLIC CHURCH believes abortion is never acceptable. It is strongly against abortion in every situation. However, it does accept abortion if it is to save the life of the mother. This is because the intention behind this action is not to end the pregnancy, but to care for the woman's life and health. The end of the pregnancy is an unfortunate side-effect.

The Catholic Church teaches that the foetus is a human being from the moment of CONCEPTION. As the Church believes that all human life is sacred the foetus has a right to life.

The Church of England

Other Christian DENOMINATIONS including the CHURCH OF ENGLAND are generally opposed to abortion, although some believe that in certain situations it can be justified. These situations include if the continued pregnancy will lead to the mother's death, or if the foetus is so badly disabled that after being born it would only live for a short period of time.

The Church recognises that, in trying to respond to severe situations with COMPASSION, individuals within the Church may arrive at different decisions on how best to respond to pregnancy as the result of rape, or when a baby is likely to be born with a disability. Some ANGLICANS may conclude that in these situations abortion is morally acceptable, and that they are acting in the way described in Matthew 7: 12 (see page 33).

The Church believes that alternatives to abortion, such as adoption, should be available and that parents in difficult situations should be supported.

'You shall not kill by abortion the fruit of thy womb.'
from The Didache, *an early Christian writing*

To discuss

1 What does the quote from *The Didache*, shown above, mean?

2 Would all Christians agree with this idea in every situation?

3 Do you agree with the quote from *The Didache*? Give reasons for your answer.

Bible bitz

Before I formed you in the womb I knew you, before you were born I set you apart.

Jeremiah 1: 5

You shall not murder.

Exodus 20: 13

So in everything, do to others what you would have them do to you, for this sums up the Law and the Prophet.

Matthew 7: 12

For you created my inmost being; you knit me together in my mother's womb.

Psalms 139: 13

Link it up

Read the news article on the right and complete the following tasks.

1 Discuss in your class why it is that the Catholic Church is 'anti-abortion'.
2 Which of the Bible quotes above do you think Catholics use to support this view?
3 Can you suggest an alternative Christian view using the Bible quotes?

To discuss

4 Using the information in the article, do you think that it would be right for someone who is anti-abortion to fundraise for Comic Relief?

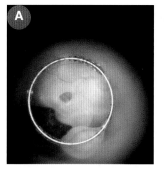

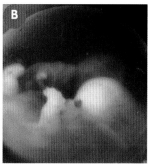

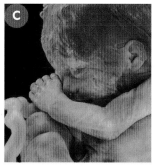

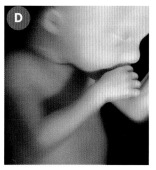

These four images show the foetus in the womb at different weeks old:
1 week (A);
7 weeks (B);
12 weeks (C);
20 weeks (D).
In the UK, abortion is legal up to 24 weeks.

TASK

1 How might someone who is PRO-LIFE (anti-abortion) use the images above to argue against abortion? What might a counter-argument be? Explain your answer.

ROW OVER COMIC RELIEF ABORTION FUNDING

A split has opened up between the Catholic Church and a pro-life group over the BBC's fundraising initiative Comic Relief.

A Catholic bishop assured people in his PARISH today that they could support Comic Relief. He explained that a ban on Catholic schools in the DIOCESE from taking part in Comic Relief was based on a misunderstanding. Since then the Church had been assured that funds raised would not go to groups supporting abortion.

Father Michael Burke, spokesman for the diocese, said: 'The Catholic faith holds all life as sacred. We are anti-abortion.' Bishop Mark Jebale added: 'I want to reassure Catholics that they can give money to Comic Relief without worrying that any funds would be given to support something that goes against Catholic teaching.'

However, the pro-life group The Society for the Protection of Unborn Children (SPUC) has expressed outrage that the Catholic Church is urging Catholics to support the appeal.

John Smeaton, national Director of SPUC, said that 'whilst Comic Relief claims that its funds are not used to support abortions and that they have even offered to hand over their books to Catholic bishops in support of their claim, the fact is that Comic Relief allocated an enormous grant of over £250,000 to the strongly pro-abortion organisation Reproductive Health Alliance Europe in the year 2001–2002'.

www.ekklesia.co.uk, 7 March 2005

Rosetta

I am totally against abortion. I am pro-life. Abortion to me means killing the innocent and everyone has the right to life.

A foetus cannot speak for itself. Mothers are given choices that are not always given to the unborn child. The rights of the unborn child are ignored, even by their mothers!

I believe that every member of the human family, whether foetus, infant or adult, is made in the image of God and is totally irreplaceable. For this and other reasons I support the Roman Catholic Church when it rejects not only abortion but also IVF, which can also be used to eliminate life.

I think it is wrong that pregnant mothers are given tests to determine the health of their babies and are given the option to abort if the baby is found to be disabled.

As a Christian, I believe that all human life has to be cherished, protected and respected.

TASK

2 Consider the following situations that may lead a woman to want to have an abortion:

▓ rape
▓ an unplanned pregnancy
▓ the foetus having developed in the womb with only one fully formed arm
▓ her own life being endangered by the continuation of the pregnancy.

Using the Christian teachings on page 32, explain whether abortion would be the morally right thing to do from the point of view of:

▓ the Catholic Church
▓ the Church of England
▓ yourself.

STRETCH WHAT YOU KNOW

'The Church of England rejects the oversimplification of the debate into "PRO CHOICE" and "pro life". At the present time in particular it believes:

- Abortion law needs to be applied more strictly and the number of abortions carried out drastically reduced.
- Every possible support, especially by church members, needs to be given to those who are pregnant in difficult circumstances.'

Abortion – A Briefing Paper, 2005, Church of England

1 In what way do you think the 'PRO-CHOICE' and 'pro-life' debate might be an oversimplification?

2 Why do you think the Church of England believes that the number of abortions needs to be 'drastically reduced'?

3 Look up the abortion briefing paper at www.cofe.anglican.org and find out what kind of support it suggests should be made available for women who are pregnant in difficult circumstances.

EXAM FOCUS...

Explain how a Christian may respond to someone who is considering having an abortion.

question d), 6 marks

...HINTS

- The keyword in this question is 'respond'. So you will need to show that a Christian might react in different ways: they might be for or against the person having an abortion – you will need to explain why linking it to a Bible or Church teaching. You will not get many marks if you just write 'A Christian would not like a person to have an abortion.' You need to say why and show how it relates to specific Christian teaching.

- It is quite important that you show the examiner that this type of question needs reference to the sanctity of life (that all life is sacred to God) and use a quote from the Bible to support this view such as Psalm 139: 13 or Jeremiah 1: 5.

- You could refer to abortion being the 'lesser of two evils' and linking compassion to the way Jesus treated people.

Christian responses to issues raised by fertility treatment

Sometimes a couple are unable to CONCEIVE naturally. This may be for various reasons, such as:

■ a woman's fallopian tubes being blocked, preventing her egg from reaching the womb
■ the man not producing healthy sperm.

It is not uncommon for a couple to be in this situation. One in six couples experience difficulty in conceiving a child at some point in their lives. In these situations they may seek alternative ways to help them to conceive, using modern medical procedures.

In vitro fertilisation (IVF) is the method used for the conception of a human embryo outside of the mother's body. In this process an egg from the woman and sperm from the man are put together in a laboratory (and so this process is sometimes referred to as creating 'test-tube babies'). If the egg is fertilised, the embryo is placed into the woman's uterus where it continues to grow. Sometimes more than one embryo is created. If this is not used, it is either destroyed or used for medical research.

In other situations, an anonymous donor is used to provide sperm or eggs. This helps to create an embryo when one person in the couple is INFERTILE, and the process is known as artificial insemination by donor (AID).

A third form of fertility treatment is when frozen embryos, sometimes produced as a result of IVF, are donated to infertile couples, thus allowing them to have a child

To discuss

1 Who do you think is creating life when fertility treatment is used?

2 Do you think it is still possible for a Christian to see God as the life giver when conception occurs through fertility treatment?

 Bible bitz

Abram said, 'O Sovereign Lord, what can you give me since I remain childless?'
Genesis 15: 2

Rachel ... said to Jacob, 'Give me children, or I'll die!'
Genesis 30: 1

Hannah had [no children] ... because the Lord had closed her womb.
1 Samuel 1: 2–6

So in everything, do to others what you would have them do to you.
Matthew 7: 12

[Jesus] welcomed them [the crowds] and spoke to them about the kingdom of God, and healed those who needed healing.
Luke 9: 11

 Link it up

Read the Bible quotes opposite.

1 For each quote, decide and explain whether or not it supports the view that every woman has the right to conceive.

2 What do the quotes tell you about what Christian attitudes towards fertility might be?

My husband and I have been married for ten years. We started trying to have a child shortly after we were married. When we didn't conceive on our own we went to the doctor. Nothing worked. I was sure I would never become pregnant. Finally, we decided to try IVF. We made the decision that if IVF didn't work that was it. We only had the money to try once. When five of the eleven eggs fertilised, I felt that was a huge accomplishment. In my mind, I had five children! Three of them were transferred and twelve days later I found out that I was pregnant.

I gave birth to a healthy, beautiful baby girl. She is the most wonderful thing I've ever created in my life. She has just started walking, and today when she was sitting on my lap she leaned over and kissed my cheek for the first time.

All those years I used to wonder and try to imagine what my child would look like. I still look at her and think, 'So this is what my child looks like.' After a year, it's still hard to believe she is actually mine.

'Medical research which involves the destruction of human embryos is a crime against their dignity as human beings.'

from The Catholic Bishops Conference, 1994

To discuss

3 Read the quote above. Do you believe that it is right to talk about embryos as human beings with dignity? Why?

TASKS

1 Read the account above. Write down the effect that fertility treatment seems to have had on the mother.

2 Do you think every woman should have the right to have a child if they want? You may find it helpful to discuss this before writing your answer down.

Christian teachings

Christians do not deny the suffering that infertility can bring to a couple. However, they are not all in agreement over the use of fertility treatment.

What does the Bible say?

Some Christians believe that God has given humans the ability to develop medical knowledge and procedures to help in situations such as infertility. Jesus is often recorded in the Bible carrying out acts of healing, brought about by his love and compassion for humankind (see for example Luke 9: 11, on page 36). These Christians believe that fertility treatment eases the suffering for many couples who otherwise could not have children; children born through such treatment are wanted and loved. To be against fertility treatment would not, they suggest, be displaying a loving attitude towards one's neighbour. The Bible is clear that we should treat others the way we too would like to be treated (see for example Matthew 7: 12, on page 36).

Does fertility treatment challenge the will of God?

Some Christians are completely against the use of fertility treatment because they believe it challenges the will of God. These Christians might argue that if God had wanted the couple to be able to conceive he would not have allowed them to be infertile in the first place. Many Christians argue that a child is a gift that is given by God, not a right that all women possess. This idea is seen in the story of Hannah in the book of Samuel in the Bible, which says that she was unable to have a child because God had closed her womb, making her unable to conceive.

Does fertility treatment involve another person in a marriage that should just be between two people?

The Catholic Church believes that the use of donor eggs or sperm, AID, is completely wrong. It believes that such treatment allows a third person into a marriage relationship when there should just be the husband and wife.

What is the status of the embryo?

Many Christians also express concern over the use or disposal of unwanted embryos created through fertility treatment. For many Christians an embryo is a human being who should be protected and treated with DIGNITY. So, in this view, to destroy an embryo or use it in research is inhumane and comparable to murder. This is another reason why some Christians are against fertility treatment.

Is there an alternative to fertility treatment for a childless couple?

Many Christians believe that the most loving act of an infertile couple would be to adopt a child who has been born and is unwanted by its natural parents.

Clinics prepare for 'lifestyle' fertility treatment

Ian Sample, science correspondent
6 January 2006, *The Guardian*

Fertility clinics are gearing up to open their doors to fertile couples seeking treatment as a lifestyle choice rather than a medical necessity, experts said yesterday.

Advances in medical techniques, which centre on safe and effective ways to preserve fertility, mean healthy people will be able to store eggs and sperm produced in their prime for use at a later date.

This new choice reflects a rise in what some fertility specialists have called the 'have it all generation' who do not want to compromise between career and family.

Research is focusing on refining techniques to freeze good quality eggs taken from women in their 20s and early 30s, as female fertility drops dramatically beyond the age of 35. But recent studies have revealed that a man's fertility also nosedives with age, driving the development of methods to keep healthy sperm on ice.

'What's going to happen, and we're going to make it happen, is that a lot of people will start using IVF who don't have a fertility problem. It will take a few years to come about, but that change will happen,' said Dr Fishel.

Only a handful of clinics in Britain offer egg-freezing services and the option is almost entirely reserved for women due to have radiotherapy for cancer or who have been through one cycle of IVF and object to having spare eggs fertilised and frozen. To date, only four babies have been born from frozen eggs in the country, all with the help of the Midlands Fertility Services near Birmingham.

There are no signs yet that egg freezing has health implications for the baby, and medical experts say the safety and success rate of the procedure is improving. In standard IVF, a fresh egg has a 25 per cent chance of leading to a successful pregnancy, but at best, frozen eggs have a 15 per cent success rate.

'When we get to the stage that frozen eggs are safe and efficient, a proportion of our society will have their eggs frozen at a younger age and then pursue their lifestyle as they should until they want to start a family,' said Dr Fishel. The treatment, costing around £2,200, could see women in their 50s implanted with their own eggs frozen decades earlier.

TASKS

Read the Christian teachings on page 38 and the article on this page.

3 Why might a fertile individual choose to use IVF in the future?

4 Does the idea of using IVF for a fertile person conflict with any Christian teachings? Why?

5 Explain to what extent you think that being able to use IVF in the way described in the news article is acceptable.

EXAM FOCUS...

Explain Christian attitudes towards fertility treatment.
question d), 6 marks

...HINTS

■ The keyword in this question is 'attitudes'. So you will need to show that different Christians will have different viewpoints on fertility treatment. Do not spend time on stating all the different types of fertility treatment unless a particular type of treatment lends itself to a specific teaching. For example, if AID (donated eggs or sperm) is used then this is a concern to some Christians because it involves a third party and this is seen as adultery and is thus breaking the seventh commandment 'Do not commit adultery'.

■ The other keyword is 'explain' and thus you will need to use the word 'because'. A Christian would be against fertility treatment because ....

■ You could refer to the sanctity of life and use a quote in support because some Christians believe life begins at conception and thus disagree with spare embryos being thrown away or frozen.

■ You could refer to the alternative option to fertility treatment: adoption, but remember to explain why this option might be preferred.

■ Remember to say why a Christian might agree with fertility treatment.

Christian responses to issues raised by cloning

What is human cloning?

There are different types of cloning which can be broken down into three main forms:

1) DNA cloning

This is the process where multiple identical copies are made of a DNA sequence and the copies are then used in many biological and technical experiments. For example the large-scale production of proteins.

2) Reproductive cloning

Reproductive cloning is used to produce an animal that has the same DNA as another animal. That is, the animal is cloned from a cell of another animal. Dolly the sheep was created in this way. The genetic material of the donor animal is transferred to an egg whose nucleus has been removed, and the embryo is subsequently transferred to a female animal to continue to develop until birth. Reproductive cloning has low success rates, for example Dolly the sheep was only one success out of 276 tries.

3) Therapeutic cloning

Therapeutic cloning, also called embryo cloning, is the production of human embryos in order to gather stem cells from them for use in research. This process takes place five days after the egg has been fertilised and destroys the embryo. Stem cells are used to study human development and disease. Many researchers hope that one day stem cells can be used to serve as replacement cells to treat heart disease, Alzheimer's, cancer and other diseases.

Dolly was the first animal to be cloned using nuclear transfer. She was cloned by Ian Wilmut, Keith Campbell and colleagues at the Roslin Institute in Edinburgh, Scotland. She was born on 5 July 1996 and she lived until the age of six.

In March 2008 a team of international scientists based at the Sloan-Kettering Institute in New York cured mice with Parkinson's disease using therapeutic cloning. The process involved using neurons grown in the laboratory that were made from their own cloned skin cells.

TASKS

1 Explain the difference between the three main types of cloning.
2 Outline the UK law on cloning.

To discuss

1 What do you think could be the benefits gained from each of the three types of cloning?

2 What conclusions could you draw about the use of therapeutic cloning based on the example in the photograph above?

3 What reasons do you think there are for not allowing reproductive cloning in the UK?

4 Based on your existing knowledge of the sanctity of life how do you think Christians may respond to human cloning?

The law on cloning in the UK

Currently therapeutic cloning is allowed under license from the Human Fertilisation and Embryology Authority. The first licence was granted on 11 August 2004 to researchers at the University of Newcastle to allow them to investigate treatments for diabetes, Parkinson's disease and Alzheimer's disease. The 2001 Human Reproductive Cloning Act bans reproductive cloning in the UK.

Christian responses

For Christians, the issue of human cloning creates many moral dilemmas. God is the giver of all life and so human life is considered sacred; for some Christians this includes human life that is still in an embryonic state. The process of discarding embryos after using them for research can be seen by some Christians as undermining their humanity. However, many Christians also recognise that God has given us our intelligence and that we should use it. Scientists have used their God-given intelligence to develop cloning and with that the possibility of using it to find many cures for human diseases. So there exists within Christianity a range of teachings and responses to the issue of human cloning.

The Catholic Church

The Catholic Church believes that research on cloned human embryos is both immoral and unnecessary. It is immoral because it involves the deliberate creation of new human life for the sole purpose of removing stem cells for research. They believe that it removes all dignity from an individual human life at the very earliest stages. The Catholic Church says that the use of human embryos for cloning reduces them to no more than a commodity. The Church does not deny the good motives behind the research using cloned embryos but it cannot condone it as morally acceptable.

The Church of England

The Church of England's Board of Social Responsibility published a briefing paper called 'Therapeutic Uses of Cell Nuclear Replacement' in 2000. Its aim was to help Christians to think through the issues of cloning for themselves.

The Church suggests that therapeutic cloning may be thought of as ethical, as it does not result in another human being. A Christian's view on cloning will largely depend on how the embryo is viewed. The paper explained that there are two possible ways a Christian may view an embryo. If an embryo's life is viewed as absolute, that is to say a full human being with all the moral status of any other human, then any use of an embryo as simply a tool is wrong. This is reflected in the Catholic stance on cloning. However, the embryo's status may be considered developmental, that is to say that it is treated with profound respect because it has the potential to develop into a human being, but that its ethical status develops as it develops. In this case it is possible to accept therapeutic cloning because the embryos are used only for the first 14 days of development. This idea is not unfamiliar in Church belief as St Thomas Aquinas held the view that the male foetus received its soul after 40 days, and a female foetus after 90 days.

In the paper the issue is raised as to whether humans are trying to play God and control life and death when using cloning. Two points are made:

1   Cloning is an act created by scientists and so may be called unnatural. However, scientists and doctors already involve themselves in many unnatural acts that Christians generally find acceptable. For example, heart transplants to save lives. Therapeutic cloning may potentially help save lives or improve the quality of human life just as transplants do.

2   The human ability to understand and change the world comes from our God-given intellect. People should use their God-given powers in accordance with God's desire for humans. This does not mean all that can be done should be done but it is important not to dismiss every advance that gives humans the ability to change human life.

TASKS

3   Using both the Catholic and Church of England responses outline two views that Christians may have towards cloning and the reasons for each view.

4   Explain whether in your opinion the use of embryo cloning is morally acceptable.

EXAM FOCUS...

'It is wrong to play God and clone embryos.'
Discuss this statement. You should include different, supported points of view and a personal viewpoint. You must refer to Christianity in your answer.

question e) 12 marks

...HINTS

■ Remember – it is important to show different points of view and also your own personal point of view.

■ This question is asking you to discuss and evaluate (look at the arguments for and against) and then come to a conclusion on whether the statement is true or false. You may not want to agree or disagree entirely – that is fine but you must support your conclusion with a valid reason.

■ This question is referring to the fact that God is responsible for the creation of life (Genesis and Job 1: 21) so you should refer to the sanctity of life and include a biblical teaching to support this idea.

■ You could refer to all or just one type of cloning in respect of this question but remember to link it up to specific Christian teachings.

■ You need to show why cloning might be acceptable to Christians.

■ You need to include your own personal viewpoint.

Christian attitudes towards euthanasia and suicide

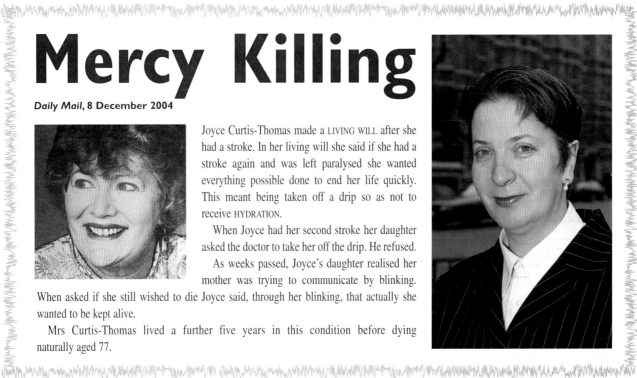

Mercy Killing

Daily Mail, 8 December 2004

Joyce Curtis-Thomas made a LIVING WILL after she had a stroke. In her living will she said if she had a stroke again and was left paralysed she wanted everything possible done to end her life quickly. This meant being taken off a drip so as not to receive HYDRATION.

When Joyce had her second stroke her daughter asked the doctor to take her off the drip. He refused.

As weeks passed, Joyce's daughter realised her mother was trying to communicate by blinking. When asked if she still wished to die Joyce said, through her blinking, that actually she wanted to be kept alive.

Mrs Curtis-Thomas lived a further five years in this condition before dying naturally aged 77.

To discuss

1 Read the article above. Do you think it is a good idea to give people the right to make living wills?

2 Do you think a person can ever be certain about what they would want in a situation like that of Mrs Curtis-Thomas? Or do you think there will always be the risk that people will change their mind?

Euthanasia

Translated literally from Ancient Greek, 'euthanasia' means a gentle and easy death. In the modern world, it refers to when a person chooses to have their life ended, usually as a response to a terminal illness, for example motor neurone disease. Many people believe that our bodies are our own and that people should have the right to do what they want with them, including euthanasia. There are two main types of euthanasia – voluntary and involuntary.

▓ Voluntary euthanasia

Voluntary euthanasia is when the person concerned asks someone else to help them die. They may persuade another person to help them to die, or, as Mrs Curtis-Thomas did, write a living will which explains their wishes if they are no longer able to communicate them. They may refuse to have the medical treatment needed to keep them alive.

▓ Involuntary euthanasia

Involuntary euthanasia comes into play when a person is no longer able to make a decision, for example by being in a coma or in a PERSISTENT VEGETATIVE STATE. The decision to allow the person to die is therefore taken by relatives or medical experts.

BB Bible bitz

Your body is a temple of the Holy Spirit.

I Corinthians 6: 19

You shall not murder.

Exodus 20: 13

There is a time for everything, and a season for every activity under heaven: a time to be born and a time to die, a time to plant and a time to uproot.

Ecclesiastes 3: 1–2

God has said: 'Never will I leave you, never will I forsake you.'

Hebrews, 13: 5

Link it up

Using the bible quotes above, identify and explain those that could be used to support the following Christian beliefs:

1. Humans do not and should not possess the right to choose to die.
2. It is acceptable to refuse medical treatment to preserve life as it allows nature to take its course, allowing someone to die.
3. God cares for each individual and knows the time for each person's death. No one has the right to kill themselves.
4. Hospices offer an alternative – they give terminally ill people the opportunity to die naturally, in comfort and dignity.

Christian teachings

The Catholic Church and The Church of England teach that euthanasia is morally wrong. They, along with other Christians, firmly adhere to the sixth commandment, 'You shall not murder'. Catholics and Anglicans apply this belief to all people including the elderly, the disabled and the terminally ill. Pope John Paul II said that people should always choose life over death. For this reason, these two denominations are against any law that legalises euthanasia in any way. Only God owns life – therefore humans do not and should not possess the right to choose to die.

Many Christians believe that suffering and pain are part of life and not a reason to devalue life or to choose death. They believe God should be trusted in all aspects of life, and that God continues to love humans in any condition (Hebrews 13: 5). Only dying naturally is truly dignified, as well as a way of showing complete faith in God.

However, both the Catholic Church and the Church of England believe that it is acceptable to refuse life-preserving medical treatment, as this allows nature to take its course. The Catholic Church also accepts death that occurs as part of what they call 'DOUBLE EFFECT'. This is when medicine is used to relieve pain, but the side-effect is to speed up the moment of death.

Christian denominations support the HOSPICE movement, which developed from the belief that people should be helped to die with dignity. Hospices are places where terminally ill people are cared for and given the opportunity to die naturally, in comfort and dignity. The Church of England has referred to hospices as places of compassion and support for the dying.

EXAM FOCUS...

Describe Christian teachings about euthanasia.

question d), 6 marks

...HINTS

- It is important to note that the question is asking for 'Christian teachings'. Therefore it is not just a matter of saying that some Christians might agree with euthanasia and some may be against it – you have to explain why using specific teachings from the Churches or the Bible.

- It would be good to refer to the sanctity of life and include a Bible teaching in support such as Genesis 1: 27; Psalm 139: 13; or Jeremiah 1: 5.

- You could refer to the sixth commandment: 'You shall not murder'.

- You could mention the alternative to euthanasia – the hospice movement – but you would need to link it to a Christian teaching.

- To help you look at the teachings above.

To discuss

3 Read Lorraine's account. What does she believe about euthanasia? Explain whether you agree or disagree with what Lorraine says.

4 Read the quote above. Do you think killing can ever be compassionate? Why?

TASKS

1 As individuals, do we have a right to choose when to carry on with life and when to die?

2 What differences are there between suicide and euthanasia?

3 Based upon what you already know about the Christian belief in the sanctity of life (see page 30), what do you think the Christian attitude to euthanasia and suicide would be?

Lorraine

I find the question of whether euthanasia is right really hard to answer. I don't think I'd ever want to end my life early and miss out on time with my friends and family. But I don't really know what it must be like to be terminally ill or in terrible pain. Maybe in that situation it would be different.

When my nan was ill with cancer she went to a hospice. The nurses there were great and she seemed to be comfortable, but she wasn't really herself. I do believe that God is with us always, and that he won't leave us without the strength to cope, whatever situation we are in. I guess continuing to live despite our suffering is an act of faith. Sometimes though I do wonder if euthanasia is actually wrong. After all, some people say it is an act of love to help end a person's suffering, and God is love.

Suicide

Sometimes, for a variety of reasons, people feel that they no longer want to live. This can lead them to commit suicide – that is, to take their own life. People who commit suicide or attempt to commit suicide are often depressed or suffering from a mental illness. With the correct support and care, this desire to try to end their life can be removed. It is illegal to help anyone to commit suicide. Suicides are therefore usually carried out alone.

Christian teaching

All Christians believe that suicide is wrong, as life is a gift from God that should be valued, and not wilfully destroyed. The Bible talks of the body being the temple of the Holy Spirit (1 Corinthians 6: 19) and Christians believe it should therefore be treated with respect.

For this reason, most Churches believe that people who do feel suicidal should receive support and guidance so that their needs are met. This is a change from the past, when people who had committed suicide could not be buried in consecrated (holy) ground because it was believed that the individual had shown no faith in God to care for them and help them.

What Quakers believe

The QUAKERS, also known as the Society of Friends, are not united on the subject of euthanasia. Some believe that people who are suffering greatly should be allowed to die if they want to. Others believe that people should care for one another and support each other's pain so that euthanasia is not needed. Some Quakers work in hospices, helping patients to receive the necessary pain relief to die naturally, but still with dignity.

In the past when other Christian denominations would not bury suicide victims in holy ground, the Quakers did. The Quakers believe that love and support should be made available to people who feel that suicide is their only option. Some Quakers are members of the Samaritans and they provide support for many people who are struggling to find a solution to their problems.

Christianity and Medical Ethics

Case Study: *The Samaritans*

The Samaritans was set up by a London VICAR called Chad Varah. He used to see people every day in his parish who were distressed but who had no one to turn to who would listen to them. He wanted to do something to help these people, and this was how the Samaritans started. The charity was initially called 'Good Samaritans' by the *Daily Mirror* in 1953, linking Chad's organisation to the Good Samaritan whom Jesus speaks of in the Bible. In the story, a Samaritan stops to help a Jew who has been robbed, even though they come from very different backgrounds.

Today the Samaritans offers a 24-hour listening service every day of the year – the service is run by volunteers. They provide completely confidential emotional support for anyone who needs it – including those people who may feel suicidal.

The Samaritans has a three-point vision for a society in which:

■ fewer people die by suicide
■ people are able to explore their feelings

■ people are able to acknowledge and respect the feelings of others. Many Christians support the on-going work of the Samaritans either by volunteering themselves or through financial donations.

To discuss

5 Look at the Samaritans' advert. Who do you think it is targeted at?

6 Do you think a Christian would agree with the Samaritan vision for society?

EXAM FOCUS...

Explain how a Christian would respond to someone who wanted to die.

question d), 6 marks

...HINTS

■ This question could be asking about someone who wanted voluntary euthanasia but could also be applied to someone who wanted to commit suicide or who wanted an assisted suicide. It would not matter how you addressed the question as long as you were clear in your explanation. You need to show what a Christian would do or how they would react and why.

■ You would need to refer to the sanctity of life and include a Bible teaching to support such as Genesis 1: 27; Psalm 139: 13; or Jeremiah 1: 5.

■ You could refer to Paul's teaching that the body is a temple of the holy spirit (1 Corinthians 6: 19) and that suicide is considered to be a moral sin.

■ You could refer to the fact that Jesus showed compassion and therefore a Christian would respond to someone wanting to commit suicide with help. They could refer the person to the Samaritans but they would understand that such a wish was due to illness and so would not respond in a negative manner.

■ You could refer to the sixth commandment and the fact that people should not 'play' God.

Christian beliefs about the use of animals in medical research

TASK

1 Draw a Venn diagram like the one shown below and brainstorm the similarities and differences between humans and animals. An example has already been given. If you are stuck use the idea bank to help you.

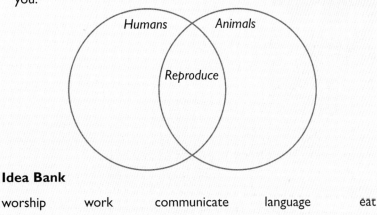

Idea Bank

worship	work	communicate	language	eat
kill	protect	conscience	relationship	

To discuss

1 Do you think humans have any responsibility towards animals? Why? Use your Venn diagram to help you answer.

2 Do you believe that either humans or animals are more important, or are they equal? Again, use the information from your Venn diagram to help you.

Animal rights activists target chain of children's nurseries linked to lab

Owen Bowcott, 29 September 2005, *The Guardian*

A chain of children's nurseries has become the target of animal rights activists who are attempting to close down the chemicals testing company Huntingdon Life Sciences, it emerged yesterday.

The directors of Leapfrog Day Nurseries, the biggest provider of childcare in the UK, received letters warning them to sever all links with HLS, which has been the subject of continued PROTESTS over its use of animals, including experiments for PHARMACEUTICAL RESEARCH.

Leapfrog, which runs 102 nurseries and was offering childcare vouchers to HLS employees, yesterday said it had received threats of physical force and that it had cut its ties to HLS.

TASKS

Read the article above.

2 What view do these protesters appear to have about the importance of animals?

3 Do you agree with the actions of the animal rights campaigners? Why?

300 people were killed or injured ensuring that no animals were harmed in any way whatsoever during the making of this film.

Medical research on animals

In the last century medical research on animals provided treatments or advancements in many areas including asthma therapy, blood transfusion, a diphtheria vaccine, drugs for high blood pressure, to control transplant rejection, heart replacement valves, penicillin and polio and whooping cough vaccine.

Dr Joseph Murray, winner of the 1990 Nobel Prize in medicine, said: 'There would not be a single person alive today as a result of an organ or bone marrow transplant without animal experimentation. All the work that we did depended on the use of animals.'

Current research includes work for multiple sclerosis, Alzheimer's disease and diabetes. Below are some animals used for research.

Armadillo
Using the armadillo, scientists have been able to develop a vaccine against leprosy, and one day these unusual South American mammals could help to provide a cure for the disease.

Guinea pig
Research on guinea pigs contributed to 23 Nobel Prizes in medicine in discovery of vitamin C, the tuberculosis bacterium, and adrenaline, as well as the development of vaccines for diphtheria and tuberculosis, replacement heart valves, blood transfusion, kidney dialysis and antibiotics.

Jellyfish
Some researchers have used jellyfish to search for an effective anti-venom to save victims of sea wasp stings, while others are studying the chemicals in jellyfish for possible use in treating cancer.

Pig
Stroke research is just one area in which pigs and miniature pigs have generated new insights. Transplanting genetically modified pig cells could hold the key to treating patients who have had a stroke, and indeed other brain disorders, such as Parkinson's disease.

To discuss

3 What point do you think the cartoon above is trying to make?

4 Using the information on this page, what do you think would be the effect of making animal experimentation for medical research illegal?

Bible bitz

God blessed them and said to them, 'Be fruitful and increase in number, fill the earth and subdue it. Rule over the fish of the sea and the birds of the air and over every living creature that moves on the ground.'

Genesis 1: 28

The earth is the Lord's, and everything in it, the world, and all who live in it.

Psalm 24: 1

Link it up

Use the Bible quotes on this page to explain what view you think a Christian might have on using animals for medical research.

1 Go to the website www.rds-online.org.uk and find out:

   a) who this group represents;
   b) what the three 'R's of medical research on animals are.

2 Explain whether you agree with the three 'R's.

To discuss

5 Explain what you think would be a Christian's response to the article on page 47.

TASK

4 Look at the two photos of animals being kept for research. For each photo explain what you believe a Christian would think about it and what actions they might take. Use the text on Christian teachings to help you decide.

Christian teachings

Christians believe that humans are the most important part of God's creation, and that God gave humans responsibility to rule over animals and control them. In the Bible, humans are referred to as temples of the Holy Spirit and are given the opportunity of salvation and a place in heaven after death. Animals on the other hand are not considered to have souls and do not have the same possibility of a relationship with God as humans do. In Mark there is a story about Jesus healing a man possessed by a demon by sending the demon into a herd of pigs.

Christians believe that as rulers over animals it is acceptable to use animals for human benefit. However, humans also have a responsibility to ensure that animals are cared for and kept in acceptable conditions and not abused or mistreated. This is because they believe everything in the world belongs to God (Psalm 24).

The Catholic Church

The Catholic Church states that 'medical and scientific experimentation on animals is a morally acceptable practice if it remains within reasonable limits and contributes to caring for or saving human lives'. However, the Church also teaches that unnecessary suffering should never be inflicted on animals.

The Church of England

In a similar fashion, the Church of England also teaches that humans have a responsibility to care for the welfare of animals, even though it may be necessary at times to use them in experiments, for example in initial medical research into a new drug or disease. When animals are used in medical experimentation the Church believes that any suffering needs to be kept to a minimum.

Pictures A and B show mice being kept in a lab for research purposes. What condition do the mice live in? Is there any difference between the two photos?

Case Study: *National Anti-Vivisection Society*

The National ANTI-VIVISECTION society (NAVS) is dedicated to abolishing the exploitation of animals in research, education and product testing.

NAVS promotes greater compassion, respect and justice for animals through educational programmes based on respected ethical and scientific theory and supported by extensive documentation of the cruelty and waste of vivisection. NAVS' educational programmes are directed at increasing public awareness about vivisection, identifying humane solutions to human problems, developing alternatives to the use of animals and working with like-minded individuals and groups to effect changes which help to end suffering.

What NAVS says about medical research

Medical research is what most people think of when they hear the phrase 'animal experimentation' or 'animal research'. Animals used in medical research are used to model human disease.

Everyone wants to see cures for diseases like Alzheimer's, Parkinson's, cancer, stroke, heart attack, AIDS, and so forth. Many people envisage these cures happening by using animals to model human disease. Is that such a bad idea?

But today we are studying human disease and human physiology on a much more fine-grained level. For example, today we know that even members of the same species react differently to the same drug and disease. For example, The National Cancer Institute (NCI) tested twelve anti-cancer drugs currently being used successfully in humans on laboratory mice. The scientists studied mice that were growing 48 different kinds of human cancers and treated them with the twelve different drugs. They found that in between 30 and 48 instances, the drugs were ineffective on the mice. In other words, in 63 per cent of the cases, the mouse models with human tumours predicted human response inaccurately.

(From the NAVS website, www.navs.org)

STRETCH WHAT YOU KNOW

Not all people share Christian views about using animals for medical experimentation.

1 Read the National Anti-Vivisection Society case study.
2 Identify three reasons that NAVS gives for opposing the use of animals for research.
3 Choose one of the three areas that you have identified and find out more about it by visiting the NAVS website.

EXAM FOCUS...

Explain Christian attitudes to the use of animals in medical research.

question d), 6 marks

...HINTS

■ The two keywords in this question are 'explain' and 'attitudes'. So make sure you show different Christian viewpoints (not your own thoughts) and that you explain why they have these beliefs. A lot of candidates lose valuable marks on this type of question because they tend to get carried away with what they believe about the use of animals in medical research. The d) part of the question does not ask you for your views – you can only show what you think in part e).

■ You might like to start your answer by explaining why some Christians believe animals to be different from human beings and use a biblical quote to support this belief (Genesis 1: 27, or Genesis 2: 7).

■ You might like to include the views of Francis of Assisi or other Christians that animals should be treated the same. You could refer to the terms 'dominion' and 'stewardship'.

■ You might like to show the benefits or otherwise of the use of animals in medical research but remember to link them to what Christians believe.

LET'S **RE**VISE

Abortion is only acceptable to save the mother's life.

Abortion is wrong and unacceptable.

Human life begins at the moment of conception.
(see Jeremiah 1: 5)

The Catholic Church

Murder is prohibited by the sixth commandment.

Life is sacred. All humans have a right to live.

Taking any human life is murder.

God will forgive such acts of abortion.

Support should be given.

Treat others the way you want to be treated.
(See Matthew 7: 12)

The Church of England

Human life begins at the moment of conception.
(See Jeremiah 1: 5)

In some situations abortion is the most loving option, e.g. in cases of rape or severe disability.

Life is sacred. All humans have a right to live.

TASKS

1 Write a paragraph on each of the two diagrams, taking each individual point and explaining it clearly.

2 Support each point with evidence or biblical references based on your earlier work on abortion.

LET'S REVISE

Christian attitudes towards euthanasia and suicide

All life is sacred, as it is given by God.

Murder is wrong. God chooses when a life will end.

Hospices provide an alternative to euthanasia.

The double effect is accepted by many Christians.

Christians believe suicide and voluntary euthanasia are unacceptable.

All life is valuable.

Although it is acceptable to refuse treatment, God is in control.

Relying on God in all situations is an act of faith.

God can help people cope in any situation.

TASKS

1   Write five questions based on the information in this diagram that would test someone's knowledge of this section.

▧   Swap questions with another person in the class and answer their questions from what you have revised.

▧   Check your answers against the diagram and correct them as necessary.

2   Create revision cards of your own for the topic 'Christianity and medical ethics'. For example, on:

▧   The Christian belief in the sanctity of life.

▧   The work of the Samaritans and why Christians may choose to support the organisation.

▧   Christian responses to issues raised by fertility treatment.

▧   Christian beliefs about the use of animals for medical research.

LET'S REVISE

a) What is euthanasia? *1 mark*

▧ A short explanation of what the term/word means is needed: for example, 'mercy killing' or 'helping someone to die because they are dying in pain'.

b) Describe Christian teachings on suicide. *2 marks*

▧ The keyword here is 'teachings' so you could give a Bible quote that would support the sanctity of life and also quote the sixth commandment 'You shall not murder'.

c) What does Christianity teach about fertility treatment? *3 marks*

▧ The keyword here is 'teach' so you will need to refer to the Bible or to the different Church teachings.

▧ You could mention some Christians would be against it and show why by including a specific teaching and then show why some Christians might agree with it by perhaps including one of the purposes of marriage.

d) Explain Christian attitudes to abortion. *6 marks*

▧ The keyword is 'attitudes' and so you will need to show different Christian beliefs about whether abortion is acceptable or not. Remember to explain the different attitudes by linking them to specific biblical views.

▧ You would need to refer to the sanctity of life.

e) 'It is wrong to use animals for medical research.'
Discuss this statement. You should include different, supported points of view and a personal viewpoint. You must refer to Christianity in your answer.

12 marks

▧ Remember – it is important to show different points of view and also your own personal point of view.

▧ This question is asking you to discuss and evaluate (look at the arguments for and against) and then come to a conclusion on whether the statement is true or false. You may not want to agree or disagree entirely – that is fine but you must support your conclusion with a valid reason.

▧ The question is asking about medical research and is not referring to eating animals. Often candidates talk about vegetarianism in such a question and this is not what the question is asking.

▧ You could refer to the fact that some Christians believe animals to be different to human beings using Bible teachings to support; or that some Christians believe that they are not different.

▧ You could refer to the terms 'dominion' and 'stewardship' using Bible teachings in support.

▧ You could refer to the benefits or otherwise of using animals.

▧ Remember to include your own opinion.

Christianity, Poverty and Wealth

Key Concepts

In this topic you will learn about:

- Christian views of wealth
- Some of the causes of poverty, hunger and disease
- Christian responses to the needs of the starving, poor and sick
- Biblical teaching about caring for others
- Different ways Christian charity is put into practice
- Christian teaching about the use of money
- Giving to charity
- Christian teaching about moral and immoral occupations.

One of the key concepts in this topic is the Christian belief that people should live their lives as good stewards, using the resources given by God to help all people achieve a reasonable standard of living. Another key concept is Christians' belief that their responsibility as stewards should extend to how they use their money and the jobs they choose to take, in order that they are not exploiting the world or other people through their occupation.

 Bible bitz

No one can serve two masters. Either he will hate the one and love the other, or he will be devoted to the one and despise the other. You cannot serve both God and money.

Matthew 6: 24

Do not store up for yourselves treasures on earth, where moth and rust destroy, and where thieves break in and steal. But store up for yourselves treasures in heaven, where moth and rust do not destroy, and where thieves do not break in and steal.

Matthew 6: 18–20

For the love of money is a root of all kinds of evil. Some people, eager for money, have wandered from the faith and pierced themselves with many griefs.

I Timothy 6: 10

Whoever loves money never has money enough; whoever loves wealth is never satisfied with his income.

Ecclesiastes 5: 10

Command those who are rich in this present world not to be arrogant nor to put their hope in wealth, which is so uncertain, but to put their hope in God, who richly provides us with everything for our enjoyment.

I Timothy 6: 17

Christian views of wealth

Christians believe that all that we have is from God and that we are stewards of it for him. This includes our wealth. In Psalm 50 God says 'the world and all that is in it is mine'. Wealth is not necessarily bad or wrong, but how Christians use their wealth is important. Christians believe that to love money and make it their goal in life is evil, as it says in 1 Timothy 6: 10. In Matthew 6, Jesus warns his disciples that money can take the place of God in their lives and that they must be careful to remain faithful to him. In response to this Christians aim to use their wealth wisely in order to be obedient to the will of God.

 Link it up

1 Explain, using the Bible bitz to help you, what you think Christians mean when they say that money should be used wisely.
2 Give reasons from the Bible bitz for using money wisely.
3 How wise do you think the Christian approach to the use of money is?

The causes of poverty, hunger and disease

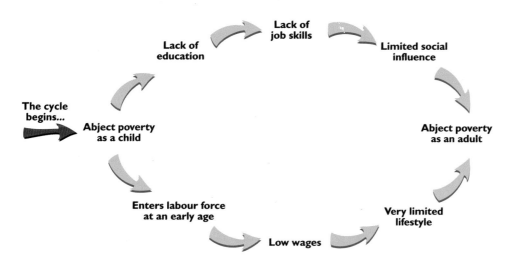

The cycle begins...

- Abject poverty as a child
- Lack of education
- Lack of job skills
- Limited social influence
- Abject poverty as an adult
- Very limited lifestyle
- Low wages
- Enters labour force at an early age

TASK

1 Use the poverty cycle diagram on the left and the statistics in the graphic to explain what you think the effects of poverty are.

Poverty is a situation of need often occurring when a person's income falls below the POVERTY LINE. The poverty line is the level of income below which a person cannot afford to buy all the resources that they need to live, such as food and clothing. In August 2008 the World Bank estimated that 1.4 billion people live below or at this line. Poverty leads to hunger, debt, disease and short life expectancy.

The richest 50 million people in Europe and North America have the same income as 2.7 billion poor people in the rest of the world.

There are 2.2 billion children in the world – 1 billion live in poverty.

Of the 1.9 billion children in the developing world:
- 640 million are without adequate shelter (one in three)
- 400 million have no access to safe water (one in five)
- 270 million have no access to health services (one in seven)

Less than 1 per cent of what was spent on weapons every year was needed to put every child into school by the year 2000. This did not happen.

Nearly a billion people entered the twenty-first century unable to read a book or even sign their name.

Some statistics on poverty

Being poor tends to result in other disadvantages, such as limited education. This may then lead to further poverty as, for example, a limited education results in less opportunity in the workplace.

A person or a family can then become trapped in a cycle of poverty, as the diagram above illustrates. Some of the causes of poverty, hunger and disease are:

- natural disasters
- education
- inadequate health care
- unfair trade
- debt
- AIDS/HIV.

Natural disasters

Natural disasters can cause extensive damage and the loss of human life. Such disasters are caused by natural events over which humans have no control, such as hurricanes, earthquakes, droughts and volcanic eruptions. Severe droughts often lead to famines and disease, as people cannot produce crops or maintain livestock without water, and lack of clean drinking water causes disease. Sudan has recently faced such a crisis, and although aid can help, starvation and massive loss of life often characterise such disasters.

Hurricanes are natural disasters which can cause loss of life and destruction of property. For example, in 2005, Hurricane Katrina hit New Orleans in the USA. The hurricane damaged the tidal barriers separating the city from Lake Pontchartrain, causing extreme flooding. Eventually the whole city was evacuated, leaving thousands homeless and without jobs or possessions. The poor of the city were left without work and unable to buy food, rebuild their houses or maintain their own health, which led to further poverty, hunger and disease.

Unfair trade

Current trade rules are unfair because they benefit rich nations disproportionately. Big businesses are able to profit from trading with impoverished countries. Unless the trade rules are made more just, rich nations will continue to grow richer at the cost of poor nations that are simply unable to compete on the global market. There are several aspects to what is considered trade injustice. These include:

■ Dumping
   This occurs when rich countries sell their own produce to developing countries, driving down the price of local produce. This makes many poor farmers even poorer.
■ Market access
   Rich countries limit and control poor countries' share of the world market by charging high taxes on imported goods. As a result, many poor countries can only afford to export raw materials, which give far lower returns than finished products.
■ Labour rights
   Companies demand faster, more flexible and cheaper production in their supply chains. For this reason many employees face insecure contracts, intense production pressure and intimidation at work.

Education

In 2000 the United Nations planned to ensure that all children of primary school age would be in education by 2015. However, there are over 100 million children around the world out of school. A lack of education restricts the opportunities available to children later in life. This then affects the skills they possess, the jobs they can do and the income that they can make.
A lack of education is therefore another direct cause of poverty, hunger and disease. Without an adequate income, families struggle to buy enough food. Undernourishment increases the likelihood of becoming seriously ill.

Debt

Debt has led to great poverty in many developing countries. Loans taken out by governments often mean that millions face poorer and poorer living standards as the resources of their country are diverted towards repaying the debt. In some instances, money has been loaned by western governments to corrupt leaders. The debt then has to be repaid even if the corrupt leaders are no longer in power. For example, shortly after freedom from apartheid (see page 106), South Africa had to pay debts incurred by the apartheid regime. What this means is that the poor are basically providing SUBSIDIES for the rich. In 2005 the developing world was spending approximately £7 on debt repayment for every 50p it received in aid.

Inadequate health care

In poorer countries health care is often not readily available, which leads to an increase of diseases that can ultimately end in widespread death. Children are left as orphans and remain stuck in poverty, unable to pay for their education and therefore limited in the work that they can do. In 2008 the World Health Organisation presented a report that said 'the poorest of the poor, around the world, have the worst health'.

TASK

2 Read about some of the causes of poverty, hunger and disease on pages 55–56 and design an information leaflet to summarise them. On your leaflet, include some statistics about the rich/poor divide where relevant (see page 55).

To discuss

Read the quote below. In what way are 'we all living with AIDS'?

'No one should
care alone.
No one should die alone.
For we are all
living with AIDS.'

*Reverend Ndungane,
Archbishop of
Cape Town (1941–)*

AIDS/HIV

In developing countries HIV and AIDS have spread dramatically in recent years. Health care and education about the causes and prevention of the disease are inadequate. The disease has so far had shattering effects on families and communities in some of the poorest countries in the world. This is evident in Sitsofe's story below.

The CHURCH OF ENGLAND believes it should speak out and act against this disease and its causes. It teaches that, as people of God, we must care for one another. It believes Christianity's response should be the same as Jesus', who met the needs of all without fear or discrimination. Jesus spent time with and healed those whom the rest of society rejected, including lepers. The Church has developed twinning links to encourage and pray for other DIOCESES in developing countries that are dealing with the reality of HIV and AIDS.

The Church of England in Africa is currently working to reduce the stigma associated with AIDS and HIV. It operates support groups for those suffering from the disease and offers training to health officers. Some specific examples of its work in Africa include:

- Nigeria – dioceses here have developed education, care and prevention programmes.
- Ghana – the Church provides HIV/AIDS awareness education and peer education in youth groups. It also links all its work to government prevention programmes.
- Rwanda – Church groups help people to buy clean and decent homes. The Church is also creating family-focused work to help change the behaviour of people of all ages to decrease the spread of AIDS and HIV.

Case Study: *Sitsofe's story*

Fifteen-year-old Sitsofe and her brother Sellasie, who is ten, live in Sokode-Etoe in the Volta region of Ghana, West Africa. Their father died eight years ago and their mother three years later. Their grandparents, Richard and Mabel Belle, look after them. Richard is 73 and going blind. The couple have lost two sons to HIV and they are struggling to find the money to care for their two orphaned grandchildren.

'Being brought up by my grandparents makes me very sad,' Sitsofe says. 'My father promised me that I would be well educated, but that promise can't be kept because he is dead. Although my friends support me and I can talk to my grandparents I feel very sorry for myself. I have lost all the happiness in life and I won't be able to achieve my ambition to be a nurse. I don't want to get married because I'm afraid of getting HIV.'

(From *Telling the Story – Being Positive about HIV/AIDS*: A Report by the Missions and Public Affairs Council of the Church of England)

TASK

3 What do you think the Church of England's response would be to Sitsofe's situation?

Christian responses to the needs of the starving, poor and sick

Christian teachings

All Christians are taught in the Bible that loving all people, particularly the most vulnerable in society, is a duty. The love Christians are expected to show is one that is caring and practical, such as giving food, money or other material things to ease others' suffering. They believe this love should be like Jesus' love: a fair love, not one making a profit from giving, but unconditional. Christians have a duty to respond in this way to others because they believe it is the way God loves each one of us.

The Church of England

The Church of England believes that it is a duty to defend weak and poor by standing up against injustices that may contribute to poverty, hunger or disease. This teaching is seen in practice through links to the Church's MISSIONARY ORGANISATIONS, its support of ONE WORLD WEEK and its work with people in local dioceses. The GENERAL SYNOD also agrees with and promotes the work of the Make Poverty History campaign. Another example is the work it is doing around the world to combat AIDS/HIV as we have seen on page 57.

The Catholic Church

The CATHOLIC CHURCH aims to show Christ's love to all people, treating each person as if they were Christ himself, just as Jesus teaches in the parable of the sheep and goats in St Matthew's gospel. In the parable, Jesus explains that when he comes in glory he will divide people into two groups: those who have cared for others by feeding, clothing and serving them – including visiting criminals in prison – and those who have not. Jesus says that treating others caringly is just as if they were caring for him, and such actions will be rewarded. The needs of the poor are important to the Church because they are important to God. The Church believes that DEVELOPED NATIONS have responsibilities towards DEVELOPING NATIONS and that their actions should be just.

STRETCH WHAT YOU KNOW

- Visit www.oneworldweek.org and find out what the theme and events are for this year.

- Explain why you think Christians might support the work of One World Week.

Case Study: One World Week

One World Week is an annual opportunity to join a worldwide movement of people taking action for justice – locally and globally. The Week comprises:

- local events to celebrate the diversity of cultures in our communities
- joining together to learn and share in caring for the Earth and its resources
- taking action for justice, EQUALITY, peace and fullness of life for all.

In 1978, One World Week (OWW) began from the desire to, for one week in every year, draw the attention to the fact that the world consists of one human race sharing one planet. Over the years it has been bringing people together to learn about global issues, and to take action locally on things having an impact on the whole world.

One World Week now involves people of many nationalities and has events all the year round. However, there is still one week in October (the week containing United Nations Day, 24 October) when the excitement is greater than at any other time.

Thousands of local groups and schools use OWW as a focus for a range of activities, events and celebrations to raise awareness and take action on issues of global justice. Each year, a small team will put together a set of web-based resources (including resources for schools) around a particular theme to inspire and assist the local activists.

(from the One World Week website)

Christian responses

Lorraine

Poverty is all around us. When I go into town or visit London I always pass people begging or living rough. Quite often on TV I see images of poverty in the developing world, whether it's another famine in Africa or the on-going consequences of the 2004 tsunami in Thailand. I have a comfortable, even wealthy, lifestyle in comparison to people in these situations. As a Christian I feel that I have a responsibility to respond to this rich-poor divide. Jesus does talk about people selling all they have and giving it to the poor. I think this means not placing money and possessions at the centre of life but being willing to use some of my wealth to help others who are less fortunate. It would be mad if I were to sell all I owned. I couldn't help others as I would then be dependent on others.

Each month I give money to TearFund and a MISSIONARY worker in the Philippines. I also give money to my church each week, part of which is distributed to various charities that we support. I believe that by giving to charity I am helping others to reduce situations of poverty around the world.

In God's eyes we are all of equal worth. We don't always see this in our world where poverty causes such divisions. I believe that each of us has a responsibility to bring equality in the eyes of God nearer to reality by giving what we can and caring for others.

TASKS

1 How does Lorraine's point of view about caring for those in poverty compare with your own view?

2 What do Lorraine's account and the article tell you about how Christians should care for the poor?

STRETCH

WHAT YOU KNOW

■ Visit TearFund's website.

1 Find out why TearFund was set up.

2 Identify what countries it is working in at the moment.

3 Choose one country and summarise the work it is doing there.

A LONG-HAUL PLIGHT

Food shortages, locusts, flash floods — it's been one of the most difficult years in living memory for people in Sahel region of West Africa, writes *Abigail Frymann*. But you've helped them through it.

Millions of people faced a crisis as their food supplies ran low. Drought and locust invasions depleted this year's grain stocks and flash flooding swept away topsoil, young crops and whole herds of livestock.

Thanks to the generosity of supporters who gave £700,000 and a further £1 million from the Disasters Emergency Committee, we distributed food to vulnerable families in Niger, Mali, Mauritania and Burkina Faso. We will continue to provide extra support to the region for the next two years.

Benaba Youma, like many other farmers, had to sell off livestock to buy food. 'We received food aid from TearFund and this enabled us to live a bit longer', he says.

A TearFund worker in Burkina Faso tells us: 'To those who have given themselves over in prayer, money and work for people they don't even know: your work will not be in vain and God will undoubtedly bless you.'

Tear Times magazine

Men collecting grain from food distributions sponsored by TearFund.

BB Bible bitz

If one of your countrymen becomes poor and is unable to support himself among you, help him as you would an alien ... so that he can continue to live among you. You must not lend him money at interest or sell him food at a profit.

Leviticus 25: 35–37

Looking at his disciples, he [Jesus] said: 'Blessed are you who are poor, for yours is the kingdom of God. Blessed are you who hunger now, for you will be satisfied. Blessed are you who weep now, for you will laugh.'

Luke 6: 20–21

If anyone has material possessions and sees his brother in need but has no pity on him, how can the love of God be in him?

I John 3: 17

TASKS

3 Describe what is happening in each picture.

4 How do you think a Christian should respond to each of the situations in the photos? Use the text on Christian teachings (page 58) and the Bible quotes above to help you.

5 Could you do anything to help people in these situations? Explain your answer.

Some of the world's poorest people live in Africa.

There's enough food for all in the world – yet in many parts of the world, like India, some people are forced to search for food in rubbish tips.

There are thousands of homeless people in the UK. In most cases, this is not their choice.

Case Study: *The World Can't Wait*

In 2005, world leaders were given a huge global mandate to make poverty history. Unprecedented public pressure led them to make some big promises – to increase aid, and cancel many poor countries' debts. By 2007, they still hadn't taken the action necessary to get rid of poverty.

In the months leading up to the 2007 G8 summit a petition calling for action to end poverty was signed by people across all the G8 nations. On Saturday 2 June 2007, as G8 leaders gathered in Germany for the G8 Summit, thousands of people met in London for The World Can't Wait rally by Westminster and the River Thames.

People from all over the UK took part in the protest alongside rock stars Midge Ure and Annie Lennox who were also supporting the protest. They posed for the press in Parliament Square with a host of 'pants to poverty' demonstrators and a giant world.

On 3 June the petition was handed over to former prime minister Tony Blair. In a written response to the campaign Tony Blair said he was pleased that the make poverty history campaign was continuing and that there had been much progress in debt reduction since the previous G8 summit in 2005. He acknowledged that the progress to get rid of world debt was not as good as world leaders had promised. In response to the ongoing campaigning he wrote:

'Without this pressure, it will take longer to end the injustices that blight the lives of millions across the globe. They are relying on you to continue to press governments to deliver on global poverty and climate change.'

Midge Ure and Annie Lennox supported the World Can't Wait Campaign

To discuss

1 Read the case study above. Tony Blair suggests that campaigns like 'The World Can't Wait' can make a difference to world poverty. How do you think they can do this?
2 Read the quote opposite. What do you think the Catholic Church believes brings true happiness?
3 To what extent do you agree with the quote?

> 'True happiness is not found in riches or well being, in human fame or power, or in any human achievement.'
>
> *Catechism of the Catholic Church*

...HINTS

- This question is asking for Christian 'teachings' so you must refer to what the Bible says or what the different Churches teach.
- There are many teachings you could use about caring for people, such as the parable of the sheep and the goats (Matthew 25: 31–46) or the parable of the Rich Man and Lazarus (Luke 16: 19–31). Remember you do not need to narrate the parable in full but refer to the meaning of the parable and show why it applies to the question.
- You could refer to 'Love your neighbour'.
- There are also teachings in the Old Testament which you could refer to, for example: Leviticus 25: 35–37. Remember, if you cannot remember where in the Bible a teaching comes from do not make it up. Also, do not panic if you cannot remember the exact words.
- To help you look at the teachings on page 58.

EXAM FOCUS...

Describe Christian teachings about concern for the poor.
question d), 6 marks

Biblical teaching about caring for others

Bible bitz

If there is a poor man among your brothers in any of the towns of the land that the Lord your God is giving you, do not be hardhearted or tightfisted toward your poor brother. Rather be open-handed and freely lend him whatever he needs.

Deuteronomy 15: 7–8

Each man should give what he has decided in his heart to give, not reluctantly or under compulsion, for God loves a cheerful giver.

2 Corinthians 9: 7

Each of you should look not only to your own interests, but also to the interests of others.

Phillipians 2: 4

Carry each other's burdens, and in this way you will fulfil the law of Christ

Galatians 6: 2

He who is kind to the poor lends to the Lord, and he will reward him for what he has done.

Proverbs 19: 17

If anyone has material possessions and sees his brother in need but has no pity on him, how can the love of God be in him? Dear children, let us not love with words or tongue but with actions and in truth. This then is how we know that we belong to the truth, and how we set our hearts at rest in his presence.

I John 3: 17–19

When the Bible was first translated from Greek to Latin the word caritas, meaning 'of high', was translated to 'agape'. Agape means unlimited loving kindness to others, just like the love of God. When translated into English the word first used was 'charity'. For example, at the end of Corinthians 13 Paul wrote of faith, hope and charity. In newer translations the word charity has been replaced with the word love. At the centre of the Christian understanding of what charity means is God's love. Giving to charity is an expression of God's love through his people. Christians are told not to be tight fisted or hard hearted but to give open handedly and freely (Deutcronomy 15: 7).

Different ways Christian charity is put into practice

Putting God's love into practice through acts of Christian charity happens in many different ways. It does include giving money to charities, but it goes beyond this. The most important thing to understand is that for Christians it is a practical expression in response to God's overwhelming love for humans. Many Christians will often give their time and sometimes even their lives to show Christian charity.

One example of Christian charity in action is the work of CAFOD, a Catholic agency which, among other things, responds to emergencies all over the world. In May 2008 volunteers operating with CAFOD gave their time and expertise to provide medicine and counselling to those involved in the Chinese earthquake that occurred in the Sichuan province. In the same way, in response to the floods in India in 2008, CAFOD used some of its charitable donations to help ensure that evacuated people were cared for.

The following examples on this page and pages 63–65 show other examples of Christian charity in practice.

World Vision (see page 72) are among a number of Christian charity organisations that work with people to help them to help themselves. Of the many projects set up in co-operation with local people their project in Cebu, Philippines, is a good example of how Christian charity is about practical help that lasts for a long time not just for a few days or years. Christians believe God's love is eternal as is his commitment to his people. In the same way Christian charity is also about commitment to people in need.

Link it up

1 Galatians 6 talks about carrying each other's burdens. What do you think is meant by this phrase?
2 Give an example from this topic of Christians carrying the burdens of others.
3 According to the Bible quotes opposite what attitude should Christians have when acting in a charitable way?
4 1 John 3 tells Christians not to love with 'words or tongue but with actions'. Why do you think this is?
5 Explain whether you think it is possible to show Christian charity without doing anything practical. Refer to the Bible bitz in your answer.

Winifred Barnes

At a church meeting I felt God was calling me to be a missionary when I was nine years old. I was not the clever one in the family but God said if I was available to him he would show me what he could do through me. Despite many difficulties I trained and qualified as a nurse and following this the Baptist Missionary Society [now called BMS World Mission] accepted me for work in the Congo.

After completing a tropical disease course at Liverpool University and a course in French I travelled to the Congo in 1940. The journey to Yakusu was 1500 km up the river by boat. Soon I was teaching the nurses, delivering babies and assisting in operations.

After four years at Yakusu I was asked to take charge of Belobo Hospital as the senior sister where I continued my work dispensing medicines and caring for people. During my time here we did

fifteen caesarean operations enabling us to save the lives of the mothers and their new-born babies. Once a week I would visit patients suffering from leprosy in huts alongside the actual hospital. It was a real privilege to get to know these men and women. I told them about a God who loves them no matter how damaged their bodies might be.

After becoming ill I spent three years back in Britain working at the Hospital for Tropical Diseases until August 1961 when I went to work as assistant matron and theatre sister in Uganda. I also spent time as acting matron at Mengo hospital in Kampala. It was a real privilege to be part of the work at this hospital. As people returned home cured we prayed that they may also have received a new life through faith in Christ. Finally on 1 July 1965 I returned home to Britain where I married and settled.

To discuss

1 How was Winifred's time as a missionary an act of Christian charity?
2 In what way was Winifred's work as a missionary similar to Jesus' life on earth?
3 Do you consider missionary work such as Winifred's a benefit to society?

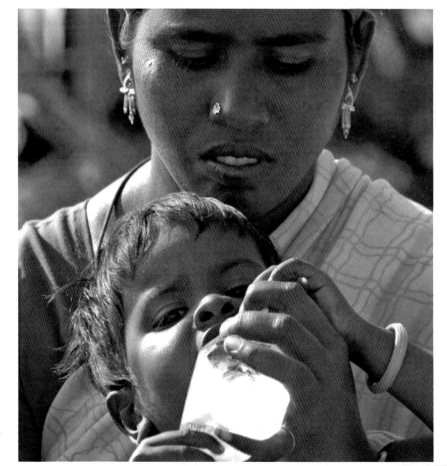

An Indian woman helps her child to drink water at a CAFOD relief camp in the south Indian city of Madras

The London City Mission (LCM) was founded in 1835 at a time when London was growing rapidly and was the largest city and port in the world. A number of Christian leaders recognised that the churches were failing to attract the people into their services and that the churches must go to the people. Dress Our Guest is one of the many acts of charity that the mission operates.

The guest spent last night on the streets of London. He wasn't partying or sightseeing, he was curled up inside a cardboard box in a doorway. Now he's inside the Webber Street Centre for homeless people, wrapping his hands around a mug of hot coffee, his senses awakened by the pungent aroma. Feeling more alert, he listens attentively to a short talk based on today's Bible passage. His brain is fully engaged but that doesn't stop his mouth watering as the smell of bacon and fried eggs wafts in from the kitchen – food for the soul will be followed by food for the body. After breakfast he will gratefully accept a shower, clean clothing and medical attention for a cut on his left hand. He'll also welcome the practical advice intended to ensure his days on the street are numbered.

The challenge is that with over 100 men coming through the centre each morning we urgently need more clothing. We give out 10,000 changes of clothes every year, all of it donated by people like you.

Can you help provide our guests with underwear, T-shirts, trousers, jumpers, socks and shoes? Why not persuade your church or youth group to join you in rising to the challenge? It needn't cost much to dress a guest: visit local supermarkets, clothing outlets and good-quality second-hand clothes shops – perhaps they'll do you a deal!

(From the LCM website: www.lcm.org.uk)

TASKS

1 Describe the charity work being encouraged through LCM's Dress Our Guest.

2 Read the Bible bitz on page 62. How is the LCM doing what it says in the Bible?

3 Explain whether you think that the Bible's requirement for Christians to show charity to others is still relevant today.

STRETCH WHAT YOU KNOW

The London City Mission (LCM) work in many areas within the city. Their mission is to share with the people of London, patiently, sensitively and individually the transforming love of God in Jesus Christ, and to enable them to join his Church.

You can find out more about their work at www.lcm.org.uk.

1 How does LCM's mission reflect the Christian idea of charity?
2 Find out and explain the core values of LCM.
3 LCM have a section on their website dedicated to prayer. In what way may some Christians believe that prayer is an important element of Christian charity?

COASTAL RESOURCE MANAGEMENT PROJECT

In 1996, with the help of the Australian government, World Vision and the United Families of Northern Cebu for Genuine Development, Incorporated implemented a community-based coastal resource management project.

Fishing in the Philippines.

The project aimed to help restore the depleted marine resources in northern Cebu and raise the standard of living. The project was completed in 1999.

For three years, 20 hectares of the sea off the coast of Luyang was declared a marine sanctuary.

World Vision provided the materials used for the installation of the artificial reefs. It also provided funds for the construction of a guardhouse and training of community members, who were mostly subsistence fishermen and labourers.

Blessed with fish and more

According to Bijoc, a community development worker at World Vision, all the hard work has paid off. 'I remember that we were greeted with resistance from the community when we were explaining to them that fishing, in any form, would not be allowed within the sanctuary,'she said.

'Amid the resistance, we proceeded with the project. Months later, the fishermen would come to us and thank us for their increased catch,' Bijoc said.

Since then, the fishermen have become more co-operative and determined to protect the sea. They organised themselves and formed the Luyang Fishermen Association. 'The project united us,' said Abayon.

Article abridged from
www.wvi.org

TASKS

Using the information and case studies on pages 62–64.

4 Explain how the work of World Vision in the Philippines is having long-term benefits.

5 Describe the different ways that Christian charity is put into practice.

6 Explain the reasons why Christians choose to act charitably.

EXAM FOCUS...

Explain why Christians might think some charities are more important than others.

question d), 6 marks

...HINTS

▪ This question is asking for examples of charities which a Christian might support but the answer should not just be a list. You need to suggest a charity, such as World Vision, and then explain why it is a charity Christians might support, but try and link the reason to a Christian teaching. So for instance, you may say that Christians would support World Vision because in the Philippines it is having long-term benefits and this is fulfilling Jesus' commandment to 'Love your neighbour' or Galatians 6 which talks of carrying each other's burdens.

▪ You could mention that some charities are an example of Jesus himself through showing compassion and caring of others.

▪ You would need to show that some charities are not considered as important as others in order to address the full focus of the question. So, some Christians might feel that animal charities are not as important and to support this you could use your knowledge and understanding of why some Christians do not believe animals to be as important as human beings.

Christian teaching about the use of money

TASKS

'Life Value Auction'

1 Look at the illustration below. Which of the items shown would you most like in your life? In small groups, carry out an auction for each item. You each have a total of £20,000 to bid on the items you want. After you have carried out the auction, answer the following questions:

▨ Which two items on the list did you most want to buy?

▨ How much would you have been prepared to pay for each of those two items? Explain why.

▨ Which items do you think give life wealth or value? Explain why.

▨ Which items do you think a Christian would give most value to?

Bible bitz

No-one can serve two masters. Either he will hate the one and love the other, or he will be devoted to the one and despise the other. You cannot serve both God and Money.

Matthew 6: 24

If anyone has material possessions and sees his brother in need but has no pity of him, how can the love of God be in him? Dear children, let us not love with words or tongue but with actions and in truth.

1 John 3: 17–18

'Go, sell everything you have and give to the poor, and you will have treasure in heaven. Then come, follow me.' At this the man's face fell. He went away sad, because he had great wealth. Jesus looked around and said to his disciples, 'How hard it is for the rich to enter the kingdom of God!'

Mark 10: 21–23

Link it up

1 Do you think it is ever practical to follow Jesus' command in Mark 10 to sell everything?

2 By looking at the other Bible quotes can you explain what point Jesus was trying to make when he gave the command to sell everything?

Christians believe that at death we can take nothing to our next life with us. They recognise that we need money to survive in the modern world, but that 'the love of money is the root of evil' (Timothy 6: 10). Christians believe that the things that give our lives value and wealth are those things given to us by God. This includes the fruits of the Spirit (Galatians 5: 22–23). The fruits of the Spirit are the characteristics Christians aim to develop because God values them. These include patience, kindness and self-control. Christians may therefore think carefully about how they use money in this life – to serve God and to respond to the needs of humanity.

Christians believe that they should be good stewards of their money, using it to care for their own families as well as for those who are less privileged. They believe money can be used for good as well as evil. However, Christians would be against using money in a way they considered morally wrong. Such uses might include buying illegal drugs or goods that have been made by exploited workers, like illegal immigrants working for very low wages.

Using money for gambling is something Christians have different views on. For example, the Catholic Church does not believe that gambling is in itself wrong. However, if gambling leads to neglect of one's responsibilities or if it becomes an addiction, then they believe that it is unacceptable. Both the Catholic Church and the Church of England believe that excessive and addictive gambling can lead to personal and social damage. Bishop Broadbent of the Church of England has said that increased gambling leads to 'the poor paying for what they can least afford'.

Case Study: *The Salvation Army*

The Salvation Army believes that gambling is motivated by selfishness and a desire for personal gain. This, they believe, goes against the Christian teachings of love, respect and concern for others. They do not believe that gambling helps someone in their life of faith or in their morality. The Salvation Army is completely against gambling and any increase of it in our society, including taking part in the National Lottery. Any member of the Salvation Army is required not to take part in any act of gambling.

STRETCH WHAT YOU KNOW

St Francis of Assisi took Jesus' teaching of giving everything you own to the poor literally, and then devoted his life to God by becoming a monk.

1 Find out who he was and what kind of life he chose by looking on the internet at www.franciscanfriarstor.com/stfrancis/

2 Write an OBITUARY in remembrance of St Francis' life.

St Peter's Basilica in Rome.

Inside St Peter's Basilica in Rome.

'A church that is in solidarity with the poor can never be a wealthy church ... it must use its wealth ... for the sake of the least of Christ's brethren'

Archbishop Desmond Tutu (1931–)

To discuss

1 Read the quote above. Why do you think the Archbishop does not believe that a church that cares for the poor can be a wealthy church?

2 What questions are raised by the images presented with this quote?

As a Christian, I believe all I have comes from God – he gives me the ability to work and he provides. Therefore, I must be a good steward of the money I have, using it as I think God wants.

Alan

This means saving and giving. I save for the future, as I believe God wants us to be responsible for ourselves. I give, aiming for the biblical guide of a tithe, at least ten per cent of my income to charity, because I believe God wants us to share with others in need and provide for the Church.

I also spend – enjoying, with my family, the good things of life that God has given. I recognise, though, that wanting money and spending can be undesirable. The Bible says that the love of money is the root of all evil – money can make us greedy, exploit others, and fail to see that the really important

things of life – peace, hope, love, joy – come from our relationship with God.

It is immoral to let money become too important to us. I do not use credit cards to buy things now – I wait until I can afford to buy the product. I do not gamble (including on the Lottery) because I believe this is being reckless with the money God has given me, and because I am not particularly interested in winning. God provides for my needs, not a lottery. I prefer to buy Fair Trade products, even if they cost more, because I know the producer is not being exploited to save me money.

I believe we have to be good stewards of what God has given. We should use money to save, give, and spend to enjoy the good life God wants for us. The use of money becomes immoral when we give it too much importance, become greedy and exploit others.

To discuss

Read Alan's view on the use of money.

3 Alan says that 'the use of money becomes immoral when we give it too much importance'. In what ways do people give money too much importance?

4 How do you think we can avoid giving money too much importance?

EXAM FOCUS...

Explain the Christian teachings about the right use of money.
question d), 6 marks

...HINTS

▪ The keyword in this question is 'teachings' so you must refer to the teachings in the Bible. You are being asked to give reasons why a Christian would want to make sure that their money is used wisely and not on immoral actions.

▪ There are many teachings you could use such as 'you cannot serve two masters' (Matthew 6: 24) or 'the love of money is the root to all evil' (1 Timothy 6: 10). Please remember that it is 'the love of' and not 'money' that is the root to all evil – this is a common mistake made by many students.

▪ Do not just put a string of Bible quotes and hope that you will then achieve full marks. You must explain the quotes in your own words to show your understanding and also make sure that you relate them to the question. So, for instance, you could say: *'A Christian would make sure that their money is not the centre of their lives and that they use it to help the poor because Paul taught that if you love money more than God then this is the root to evil.'*

▪ To help you look at the teachings on page 67.

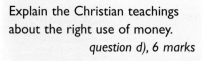

Giving to charity

Giving to charity may not simply be about giving money; it could involve a person giving their time and skills to help the charity in their work. Christians support a whole range of charities, and the ones they support reflect their values and beliefs. These may include charities that are not themselves Christian, for example Oxfam. However there are also many charities inspired by Christianity that work around the world, like Christian Aid, BMS World Mission and World Vision.

Case Study: *Christian Aid*

Christian Aid is a charity that works throughout the developing world regardless of religion or race. It was set up by Churches in the UK and Ireland in 1945. Christian Aid aims to help people to find solutions to their own problems by supporting local organisations.

One way in which Christian Aid directly helps people in developing countries is through their recent initiative of Present Aid. The gifts that people buy through Present Aid are unusual, they include a teacher's monthly salary for £45, tooth extraction for £11 and even looking after two children in a malnutrition ward for £860. The idea behind Present Aid is that people buy a gift for a friend that actually goes to someone in the developing world. A card explaining this gift is then sent to the friend that it was bought for.

You can find out more about the current work of Christian Aid by going on their youth website at www.globalgang.org.uk.

TASK

1 Read the Christian Aid case study.

   Design a sales leaflet for Present Aid promoting the idea of buying a gift for a friend that benefits someone in a developing country.

   Include some bestsellers on your leaflet. These could be those items mentioned in the case study, or you could visit Christian Aid's website to find out about some other present ideas.

Why just have turkey this Christmas?

£35

£60

A herd of goats will provide milk to drink, manure to fertilise crops, and little goats to sell on. They really are 'the gift that keeps on giving'.

£24

Ducks help families in Bangladesh hit by floods to recover, by providing eggs and a source of income.

£27

Pigs can change lives in Nicaragua by providing food, as well as more piglets which can be sold on.

This Christmas, you can have turkey, ducks, pigs, goats and even a water buffalo. They'll go to people who really need them, and help to change lives not just at Christmas, but forever. Meanwhile you'll get a beautiful card to give to the lucky recipient, telling them how the Present Aid gift you've bought on their behalf will change people's lives. Now that's a Christmas with a difference.

Order by 15 December to receive your Present Aid cards in time for Christmas Eve – and receive a free Present Aid 2009 Calendar!

christian aid

A006817

Visit presentaid.org/xmas or call 0845 330 0500 for a huge range of different gifts that make a difference.

'Ethical' presents are a great way to help those in need while giving to your loved ones at the same time.

2 Look at the advert opposite.

- Imagine you are a Christian writing a letter of application to join a BMS World Mission Action Team for your gap year.
- In your letter explain why you want to help people in the developing world.
- Use the Church teachings from pages 67 and 73 to help you write your letter.

God is changing lives throughout the world and by going short-term with BMS World Mission you can be involved. Giving a hug to a child who lives on a rubbish dump in India; carrying out a cataract operation to give sight back to a Bangladeshi; performing Christian drama on the streets of Genoa; living and working alongside Brazilian team members in Peru; developing agricultural projects in Nepal – these are just a taste of the opportunities we have for you to serve overseas. But beware, it's not only the lives of those overseas God is changing – going on short-term mission could change your life forever.

"It's given me a heart for mission and a greater perspective on the world." HANNAH, INDIA 2003-04

The range of short-term programmes makes it possible for people from a wide variety of ages and backgrounds to get involved in world mission with BMS. From filling a gap year, to doing something different with your summer holidays or using your skills to help people in need – we have a programme to suit you. Let BMS give you the opportunity of stepping out and putting your faith into action.

"Following the impact and work of the team, there is now a teenage group coming to church and two have been baptised. The team was so important..." OVERSEAS HOST, BRAZIL 2003

Interested?

Available shortly, our brand new guide to short-term mission opportunities contains further details. Request your copy now, by contacting Anna Wordsworth on 01235 517653 or volunteers@bmsworldmission.org

STRETCH WHAT YOU KNOW

Find out about the living conditions of the people from one of the countries mentioned in the advert. You could then incorporate this information into your letter of application. You could use www.24-7prayer.com/ow/ to start your research.

Case Study: *World Vision*

World Vision is a Christian charity. One of its campaigns offers people the chance to sponsor a child in the developing world. Sponsoring a child means giving a minimum monthly amount of money (£18) to World Vision. This money is then used to help the child that is being sponsored and their community. At Christmas and birthdays the sponsors are sent cards to sign and given the opportunity of making an extra donation for a present. During the course of a year, sponsors can write to their child and send gifts; the sponsored child is helped to write back by World Vision workers. People who sponsor children often feel a real sense of being able to make a difference. Sponsors often develop strong links with the person they are supporting as it is a relationship that ideally lasts until the child is at least sixteen. Some sponsors even manage to visit the child they are supporting in his or her own country.

World Vision use the money from sponsorship to help the child and their community in the best possible way. This may be to support their education, help provide fresh water or to develop farming programmes in their community.

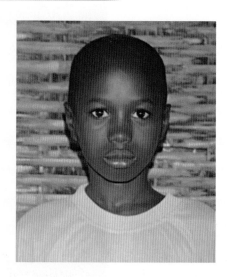

Adama

Age:	11 years old.
Home:	Senegal, near the border with Guinea Bissau.
Family:	Mother and father are farmers, cultivate groundnuts and maize.
	Four brothers.
	Three sisters.
Interests:	Football.
Ambitions:	To be a teacher.

TASKS

3   Adama is a child sponsored through World Vision by a school in the UK. If you were to meet Adama, what questions would you ask him to find out more about where he lives and his lifestyle?

4   Using the internet and library, find out more about Senegal, its people and their lifestyles. Use your research to write out a short dialogue between yourself and Adama that could be performed to the rest of your class.

Bible bitz

On the first day of every week, each one of you should set aside a sum of money in keeping with his income, saving it up.

1 Corinthians 16: 2

As he looked up, Jesus saw the rich putting their gifts into the temple treasury. He also saw a poor widow put in two very small copper coins. 'I tell you the truth,' he said, 'this poor widow has put in more than all the others. All these people gave their gifts out of their wealth; but she out of her poverty put in all she had to live on.'

Luke 21: 1–4

[W]hen you give to the needy, do not let your left hand know what your right hand is doing, so that your giving may be in secret. Then your Father, who sees what is done in secret, will reward you.

Matthew 6: 3–4

He who gives to the poor will lack nothing, but he who closes his eyes to them receives many curses.

Proverbs 28: 27

Link it up

1 From the Bible quotes above discuss what attitude you think God wants people to have when they give money to charity.

2 How do you think the Bible quotes suggest a Christian should organise their giving?

Christian teachings

Christians give to charities in many different ways. In the Old Testament, the Levites, who were priests, were given tithes from people in return for their work. In the same way, some Christians believe they should give ten per cent of their income to their church. This is known as tithing. Churches often set aside part of people's offerings to give to Christian charities that are separate from the Church itself, for example Christian Aid or CAFOD.

Christians often set up direct debits to maintain regular monthly giving to a charity or church. This helps the charity to plan their work in advance, knowing that certain amounts of money will be provided.

Charities often also provide money boxes that people can keep at home and put their change in.

It is possible to fill in a Gift Aid form when giving money to charity. This enables the charity to claim the tax back on the gift that is given, which means the charity receives more money.

EXAM FOCUS...

Explain how Christians might work to help those who are poor and suffering.

question d), 6 marks

...HINTS

■ The keyword in this question is 'how'. It is asking you to explain what a Christian would do to help someone who is poor or suffering.

■ There are many ways in which you could address this question. You could refer to giving money to a charity and so you would need to give the names of some charities a Christian might support, giving at least one Christian charity. You would then need to link this response to a Christian teaching if you can.

■ You could refer to a Christian doing active work to help someone who is poor or suffering and try and link that to a specific Christian teaching.

■ Do not just make a list of things a Christian might do – remember to link the actions to Christian beliefs.

Christian teaching about moral and immoral occupations

To discuss

1 When you finish your education what career would you like to go into and why?

2 Are there any jobs that you would refuse to do because you think they are wrong? Why?

Neither the Bible nor the Churches list occupations that a Christian must not do. However, Christian beliefs and values may affect the job they choose to do.

Christians believe that humans have a responsibility to care for one another, to protect the weak, to work the land to provide resources, but at the same time protect it. Christians also believe that they have authority over animals and that they can use them to maintain their livelihoods. This is because Genesis states that man is to rule over animals and use them for food. However, humans must care for animals and not drive them to extinction as they are a valuable part of God's creation.

These beliefs may lead a Christian to choose a caring profession such as becoming a vet, a police officer or an environmentalist. Christians are unlikely to choose a career that exploits people or encourages people to misuse resources. For this reason Christians would be unlikely to make their living working for a company that uses cheap labour in a developing country. Careers that directly harm the environment or that exploit animals are unlikely to be appropriate for a Christian.

Many Christians prefer not to work on a Sunday. This is because it is the day they set aside for worship with other Christians. The first followers of Jesus in the Bible would meet on Sundays, and Christians have largely kept this tradition. Also, in Genesis, God rested for one day after creating the world. Many Christians follow this same principle for Sundays.

TASKS

1 Identify what jobs you think are being suggested in each of the pictures on page 75.

2 Do you think a Christian might choose not to work in any of the jobs you have identified? Give reasons for your answer. Use the Christian teachings above to help you write your response.

EXAM FOCUS...

'A job is a job – it does not matter how people earn their money.'
Discuss this statement. You should include different, supported points of view and a personal viewpoint. You must refer to Christianity in your answer.

question e), 12 marks

...HINTS

■ Remember – it is important to show different points of view and also your own personal point of view.
■ This question is asking you to discuss and evaluate (look at the arguments for and against) and then come to a conclusion on whether the statement is true or false. You may not want to agree or disagree entirely – that is fine but you must support your conclusion with a valid reason.
■ You could start your answer by explaining that Christians believe they have the responsibility of 'stewardship' and that they have strict beliefs about the right use of money.
■ You could refer to specific jobs a Christian would do/not do but make sure you do not just give ideas but that you explain them and link them to Christian teachings/beliefs.
■ Then give your own personal viewpoint.

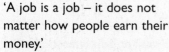

LET'S **RE**VISE

Christian teaching about concern for the poor

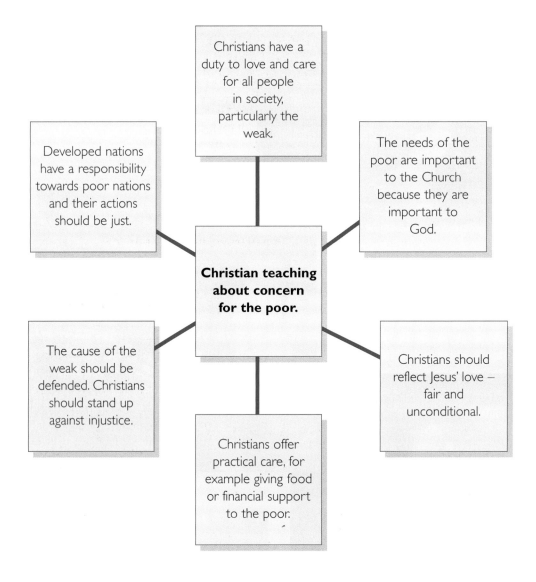

Christians have a duty to love and care for all people in society, particularly the weak.

The needs of the poor are important to the Church because they are important to God.

Developed nations have a responsibility towards poor nations and their actions should be just.

Christian teaching about concern for the poor.

The cause of the weak should be defended. Christians should stand up against injustice.

Christians should reflect Jesus' love – fair and unconditional.

Christians offer practical care, for example giving food or financial support to the poor.

TASKS

1   Write five questions based on the information in this diagram that would test someone's knowledge of this section.

2   Swap questions with another person in the class and answer their questions from what you have revised.

3   Check your answers against the diagram and correct them as necessary.

LET'S **RE**VISE

Giving to charity in Christianity

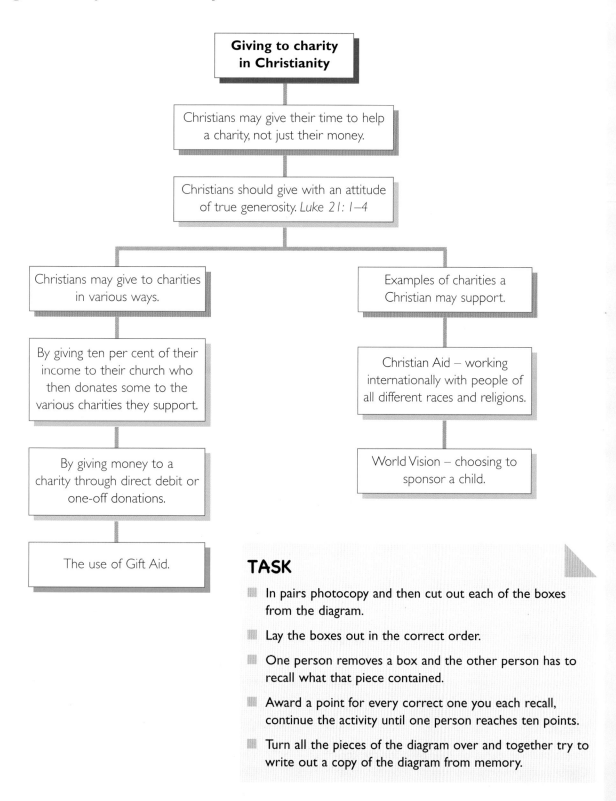

Giving to charity in Christianity

Christians may give their time to help a charity, not just their money.

Christians should give with an attitude of true generosity. *Luke 21: 1–4*

Christians may give to charities in various ways.

By giving ten per cent of their income to their church who then donates some to the various charities they support.

By giving money to a charity through direct debit or one-off donations.

The use of Gift Aid.

Examples of charities a Christian may support.

Christian Aid – working internationally with people of all different races and religions.

World Vision – choosing to sponsor a child.

TASK

▥ In pairs photocopy and then cut out each of the boxes from the diagram.

▥ Lay the boxes out in the correct order.

▥ One person removes a box and the other person has to recall what that piece contained.

▥ Award a point for every correct one you each recall, continue the activity until one person reaches ten points.

▥ Turn all the pieces of the diagram over and together try to write out a copy of the diagram from memory.

LET'S REvise

Christians teaching about moral and immoral occupations

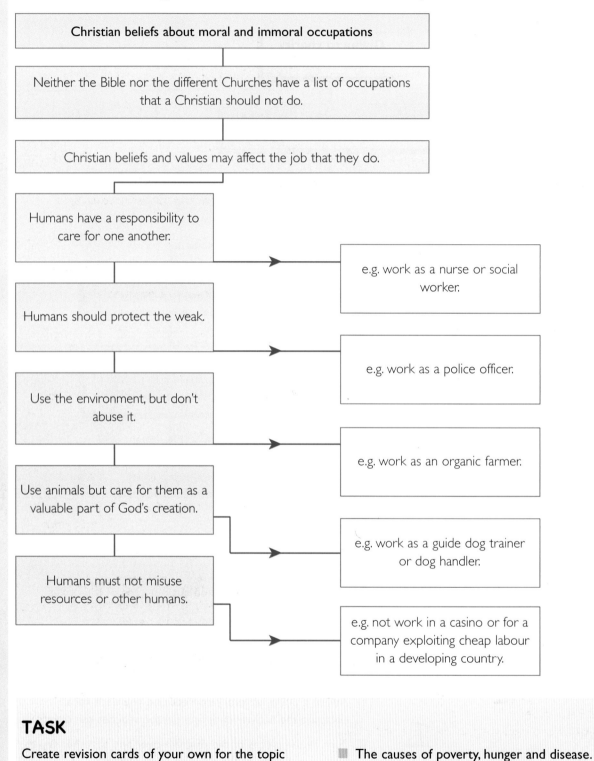

Christian beliefs about moral and immoral occupations

Neither the Bible nor the different Churches have a list of occupations that a Christian should not do.

Christian beliefs and values may affect the job that they do.

Humans have a responsibility to care for one another.

Humans should protect the weak.

Use the environment, but don't abuse it.

Use animals but care for them as a valuable part of God's creation.

Humans must not misuse resources or other humans.

e.g. work as a nurse or social worker.

e.g. work as a police officer.

e.g. work as an organic farmer.

e.g. work as a guide dog trainer or dog handler.

e.g. not work in a casino or for a company exploiting cheap labour in a developing country.

TASK

Create revision cards of your own for the topic 'Christianity, poverty and wealth'. For example:

▥ The work of Christian Aid.

▥ The causes of poverty, hunger and disease.
▥ Christian teachings about the right use of money.
▥ Giving to charity in Christianity.

LET'S REVISE

a) What is meant by the word 'charity'? *1 mark*

■ A brief explanation of the word is all that is required. So you could state it is 'giving money' or refer to the fact that sometimes it means 'an organisation' or refer to Paul's meaning of the word 'love' (1 Corinthians 13).

b) What careers would a Christian consider to be good? *2 marks*

■ This question requires you to give two examples of occupations/jobs which a Christian would consider doing, with a short explanation as to why. You could link a career to a Christian teaching.

c) What do Christians believe about gambling? *3 marks*

■ This question is asking about Christian beliefs so you would need to link your response to a Christian/biblical teaching.
■ To help you look at the teachings on page 67.

d) Explain why Christians might give money to a charity. *6 marks*

■ You would need to link your ideas to specific teachings.

e) 'Everyone should give to charity.'
Discuss this statement. You should include different, supported points of view and a personal viewpoint. You must refer to Christianity in your answer. *12 marks*

■ Remember – it is important to show different points of view and also your own personal point of view.
■ This question is asking you to discuss and evaluate (look at the arguments for and against) and then come to a conclusion on whether the statement is true or false. You may not want to agree or disagree entirely – that is fine but you must support your conclusion with a valid reason.
■ The keyword in this question is 'everyone'.
■ You would need to refer to Christian teachings when stating that Christians believe in giving to charity.
■ Think about why sometimes people cannot give to charity or why some charities might not promote Christian beliefs.
■ Remember to include your own personal view.

TOPIC 4

Christianity, Peace and Justice

Key Concepts

In this topic you will learn about:

- The Just War theory
- Christian attitudes towards war
- Christian attitudes towards the use of violence and pacifism
- The Christian concept of justice
- Crime and punishment
- Christian beliefs about and responses to social injustice.

One of the key concepts in this topic is that Christians believe violence should never be the first way of dealing with a situation. Some Christians do believe violence may be necessary at times as a last resort; other Christians are completely opposed to violence in any situation, believing it goes against the command to love that is given to Christians in the Bible. Another central concept is the Christian belief that anyone who acts against the law has to be punished. However, not all Christians agree on the way in which this should happen. There are examples from around the world where people are wrongly punished or treated unfairly, having their human rights violated. Christians oppose any such acts of social injustice.

The Just War theory

Thomas Aquinas, a thirteenth-century Christian monk and theologian, thought that there were three conditions that would make a war just or fair:

1 The war must be started by the sovereign authority, for example the government.
2 There must be a good reason to go to war, for example to protect people.
3 Everything must be done to make sure good instead of evil comes from the war.

Later on, three more conditions were added to this:
4 The war must be the last resort; every other way of solving the situation must have been tried and failed.
5 The force used must be no more than is necessary to win, and civilians or those not posing a threat, for example children, should not be targeted.
6 There must be a reasonable chance of success.

To discuss

1 Identify the wars shown in the images on page 80. Answers on page 139.
2 What do you think were the causes of each war?

To discuss

3 Was the Second Gulf War just? Work through each of the six conditions to help you structure your answer.

Case Study: *The Second Gulf War*

In late 2002, the American and British governments believed Iraq was developing weapons of mass destruction. The Iraqi government denied these claims and allowed United Nations weapons inspectors into Iraq to search for evidence of such weapons. In March 2003, the American and British governments asked UN weapons inspectors to leave and declared war on Iraq. On 9 April 2003 the government of Iraq was toppled. The UN did not support the declaration of war.

By the end of 2003, Saddam Hussein, Iraq's former president, had been captured. He had been a cruel dictator who had ordered many crimes against his own people. Since then, Iraq has held democratic elections and a new government has been formed. However, unrest still continues and no weapons of mass destruction have ever been found.

The war has cost the lives of thousands of Iraqi civilians and those of many British and American soldiers, volunteers and civilian workers. At the time of writing, foreign troops still remain in Iraq to help keep control.

Christian attitudes towards war

'Peace was not
made for the
sake of justice,
but justice
for the sake
of peace.'

*Martin Luther King
preacher and activist,
(1929–1968)*

To discuss

1 Read the quote above. What do you think Martin Luther King means when he speaks of 'justice for the sake of peace'?

2 Does Christianity see war as an act of justice?

Christians do not believe that war can be easily justified. Unless a proposed war meets all the criteria of a just war (see page 81), they usually believe it should be avoided. Christians believe that the Bible teaches the need to aim for peace and to maintain justice, but, at times, war may be necessary to achieve this. St Augustine, a theologian from the fifth century, even went as far as saying that wars that aimed to punish evil were peaceful acts.

All Churches believe that the global community should do all it can to ensure that all nations co-exist peacefully. This may include forgiveness between nations to overcome differences that might otherwise lead to war.

The CATHOLIC CHURCH teaches that peace is possible and that Christians have a duty to aim for peace in the world. Peace must be built on truth, justice, love and freedom.

Most Christians agree that war is always regretful, as it signals that other peaceful means of solving a situation have failed.

When conflict occurs, they believe that they have a responsibility to pray for all those involved to be enlightened by God's guidance and wisdom.

Some Christians are pacifists, and they do not think that war is right under any circumstance. They hold this view because they do not believe that going to war fits with the Christian teaching on love. This teaching includes love for our enemies and those who PERSECUTE us (Matthew 5: 44–45, see page 84).

STRETCH WHAT YOU KNOW

Love towards oneself remains a fundamental principle of Christian morality. Therefore it is legitimate to insist on respect for one's own right to life. Someone who defends their life is not guilty of murder, even if they are forced to deal their aggressor a lethal blow.

'If a man in self-defence uses more than necessary violence, it will be unlawful: whereas if he repels force with moderation, his defence will be lawful'

from the Catechism of the Catholic Church

1 Explain why the Catholic Church teaches that defending your own life by killing another does not make a person guilty of murder.

2 How do you think this teaching will affect a Christian's view on soldiers going to war?

Legitimate defence is not only a right, but also a serious duty for those responsible for the lives of others. Defending the common good requires that an unjust aggressor be rendered unable to cause harm. For this reason, a legitimate authority (such as the government of a country) has the right to use weapons to stop aggressors from harming the civil community.

3 What does the Catechism say is required for the defence of the common good? How does it accept that this might have to happen?

4 Explain whether you agree or disagree with this reading.

Wayne

I joined the Royal Marines on 14 October 1996. It was an exciting and scary time all rolled into one, and I knew that it was going to be the hardest thing I had ever done. Not just physically and mentally, but also, and most importantly to me, spiritually. Being a born-again Christian is to me the most important thing in my life, so I knew the test of my faith was on its way in the form of the Commando Training Centre Royal Marines (CTCRM). The Royal Marines' training barracks near Exmouth on the river Exe is where the toughest and longest recruit training in the world takes place, all to win the coveted 'Green Beret'.

A career in the Armed Forces as a Christian can be a difficult one, but it is possible if you know God has called you there. Strong influences can be a constant sidetrack, as can peer pressure, but a strong faith and belief in what you know is right will help. More importantly though, a firm and active relationship with God is a must. He is the only one who is always with me no matter what part of the world I'm in or in what situation I might find myself. He has never left me once.

I know God wants me to be a soldier, even though at times this may mean fighting the enemy. I see this part of my role as one of protecting the weak and working for peace when nothing else has achieved it. Unfortunately, to get or defend peace we sometimes have to fight for it. I believe Jesus is the Prince of Peace, and the work I do is for him.

To discuss

3 Wayne says that 'to get or defend peace we sometimes have to fight for it'. What do you think he means by this?

EXAM FOCUS...

Explain how a Christian would respond to war.

question d), 6 marks

...HINTS

■ The keyword in this question is 'respond' so make sure you link your ideas of how a Christian would respond to war to a biblical quote or the Just War theory.

■ There are different approaches to this – you could refer to the QUAKERS and say that they would never fight, linking this idea to Christian beliefs on non-violence.

■ However, it is probably easier to say that although most Christians do not believe in war there are times when it is the 'lesser of two evils' and then support the reasons why a Christian would go to war with specific biblical teachings from the Old Testament and reference to the Just War theory.

Christian attitudes towards the use of violence and pacifism

Bible bitz

Then the Lord said to Joshua, 'Do not be afraid; do not be discouraged. Take the whole army with you, and go up and attack Ai. For I have delivered into your hands the king of Ai, his people, his city and his land.'

Joshua 8: 1

Love your enemies and pray for those who persecute you, that you may be sons of your Father in heaven.

Matthew 5: 44–45

Blessed are the peacemakers, for they will be called sons of God.

Matthew 5: 9

If it is possible ... live at peace with everyone. Do not take revenge, my friends, but leave room for God's wrath ... 'If your enemy is hungry, feed him; if he is thirsty, give him something to drink. In doing this, you will heap burning coals on his head.'

Romans 12: 18–20

Pacifism

Pacifism is the belief that any use of violence is wrong. This includes any act of war. Many people choose to be pacifists because they believe there is always a way to solve a problem without violence. Pacifists believe that violence and aggression should not be tolerated, and also that further violence is not the way to eliminate them. Pacifists aim to use peaceful methods to resolve conflict instead of war. These may include SANCTIONS, PROTESTS and BOYCOTTS. Some Christians are pacifists because it says in the Bible that God requires us to love one another, including our enemies.

Christian teachings

Some DENOMINATIONS, including the Catholic Church and the CHURCH OF ENGLAND accept that sometimes war is necessary to achieve peace. Neither of these Churches promotes the use of violence, but they recognise that there are times when it may be necessary to use force as a last resort, for example for defence. There are several examples in the Old Testament when God tells his people to prepare for war. For example, when God tells the Israelites to destroy those tribes who are living in the land that he has promised to them (Joshua 1: 6). The Bible does, however, give Christians the task of aiming for peace and seeking a time when people will not fight against each other any more. The Catholic Church and Church of England aim to reflect this in their teaching.

Link it up

1 What message do you think these Bible quotes give about the importance of peace?

2 Explain what is meant when the Bible quote from Romans 12 speaks of heaping burning coals on the head of an enemy.

'War can only be got rid of through war, and in order to get rid of the gun it is necessary to take up the gun.'

Mao Zedong, founder of the People's Republic of China (1893–1976)

'Peace cannot be achieved through violence, it can only be achieved through understanding. '

Ralph Waldo Emerson, a nineteenth-century philosopher (1803–1882)

TASKS

Read both of the quotes on the left.

1 What does each mean?

2 Which one do you agree with most and why?

> 'Non-violence
> is the greatest
> force at the disposal
> of mankind. It is
> mightier than the
> mightiest weapon of
> destruction devised by
> the ingenuity of man.'
>
> *Mahatma Gandhi, non-violent
> leader of Indian
> independence
> (1869–1948)*

To discuss

Read the quote from Gandhi.
1 In what way could non-violence be used as a weapon?
2 To what extent do you agree with Gandhi's view?

TASKS

3 Why might you think that the person in the picture is a pacifist?

4 To what extent do you agree with pacifism?

Brian Haw, an anti-war demonstrator, started his protest in Parliament Square on 2 June 2001. He is still there today.

Quakers

The Quakers believe that it is never acceptable to use violence. Jesus taught that Christians must love all people, even their enemies. The Bible makes it clear that Christians must also pray for those who persecute them. These teachings lead Quakers, as well as some other Christians, to believe that violence against another person, for whatever reason, is wrong as it is not compatible with their understanding of the biblical teaching on love.

Quakers seek and suggest peaceful methods to deal with situations rather than resorting to war. They believe that governments should focus on gradual disarmament, the rule of law and fair trade laws. For example, in the Quaker document called *Think Peace* it is pointed out that 'the UK is currently spending £30.8bn on the military compared with £6bn on foreign affairs and overseas aid combined. This emphasis on national military has the counter-productive effect of generating global insecurity.' Quakers also refuse to take part in violence, so at times of war they resort to being CONSCIENTIOUS OBJECTORS, refusing to fight but accepting other roles, such as ambulance drivers. By doing this, they believe they are standing up against violence and challenging those who think it is acceptable.

EXAM FOCUS...

'Violence should never be used to solve a problem.'
Discuss this statement. You should include different, supported points of view and a personal viewpoint. You must refer to Christianity in your answer.

question e), 12 marks

...HINTS

■ Remember – it is important to show different points of view and also your own personal point of view.

■ This question is asking you to discuss and evaluate (look at the arguments for and against) and then come to a conclusion on whether the statement is true or false. You may not want to agree or disagree entirely – that is fine but you must support your conclusion with a valid reason.

■ You might like to use biblical quotes from both the Old and New Testament to show that violence should or should not be used.

■ You might like to refer to specific Christian individuals who believe that violence is not the way or even some Christians who have felt that there was no other option but to use violence.

■ Remember to include your own personal opinion.

The Christian concept of justice

To discuss

1 Can you describe any examples from history of people who have spoken out for others to bring about justice? For example, what do you know about the work of William Wiberforce, Martin Luther King or the Make Poverty History campaign?

2 How important do you think it is to have people like this in today's society?

3 Can you think of examples of justice in our world today that follow the pattern of punishment, repentance and reformation? Maybe consider the discipline policy in your own school or the way criminals are treated.

4 Christian justice speaks about defending the weak and setting the oppressed free. Do you think Christian justice may ever require the use of force or violence?

The Bible teaches Christians about God's justice. Psalm 97: 2 says that righteousness and justice are central to who God is. It is against a perfect standard that God measures all human acts so that he can respond with justice. The Bible teaches that humans are unable to lead lives of perfection but that forgiveness is part of God's system of justice. Any penalty for failing to meet God's standard of perfection is paid for through the acceptance of Jesus' sacrifice on the cross.

In the Bible, God judges, condemns and punishes those who abuse others. He has COMPASSION for those who suffer injustice, defends the weak and afflicted and sets the OPPRESSED free.

Christian justice is not simply about love and forgiveness, it demands that wrongdoing is appropriately punished and that forgiveness is only offered if the wrongdoer is repentant. In Christian justice someone who has REPENTED is given the chance to reform and move on. This approach to justice is a reflection of the way Christians believe God has dealt with the wrongdoings of humans against him. Christians believe this to be the perfect example of justice.

Christians attempt to apply the biblical teaching on God's justice in the world; this effects their attitudes towards crime and punishment, violence, war and acts of social injustice.

TASK

Read the caption opposite. What principles for human justice could be taken from the way in which God has responded to human sin?

A depiction of the crucifixion of Christ. Christians believe God accepted the death of Jesus as the punishment for human sin. As the punishment has been paid, humans can be forgiven and given help through the Holy Spirit to lead lives which are pleasing to God. Christians remember God's loving justice when they celebrate communion.

Crime and punishment

TASK

Worst crime possible

Serious crime

Minor crime

Not a crime

- Draw a line and labels as shown.
- Place each of the following crimes on the line to show how serious you believe them to be.

A Rape
B Taking paper from work to fill your printer at home
C Murder
D Robbing a bank
E Driving drunk
F Accidentally knocking a cyclist off their bike resulting in their death
G Assisting someone to end their life, on their request, because they have a terminal illness

- Now explain why you have put each crime at that point on the line.
- Discuss your answers as a class. Are there differences in your responses?

To discuss

1 Which of the four aims of punishment do you think the death penalty achieves?

2 Do you think any of the crimes from the task deserve the death penalty? Give reasons for your answer.

The aims of punishment

In the task on the left, you are asked to make judgements about a range of actions, all of which break the law. When considering punishment, the seriousness of a crime should be taken into account. Christians usually believe that the punishment of crimes has four main aims:

1 **Retribution** – a way of making sure that people, particularly victims, are able to see that the criminal has paid the price required for committing the crime.
2 **Reformation** – a chance for the criminal to reflect on what they have done wrong and to then improve their behaviour.
3 **Protection** – a security measure to ensure that the rest of society is protected from criminals who may want to harm them.
4 **Deterrence** – a way of putting people off committing a crime because of the fear of the consequences. Punishment is aimed at putting people off wanting to break the law.

Christian attitudes towards capital punishment

Capital punishment, or the death penalty, makes the criminal pay for the crime committed with his or her life. It is no longer used in the UK, but it is used regularly in parts of the USA for the most serious crimes, such as pre-meditated murder. Death by capital punishment is brought about either by using the electric chair or, more commonly, by using a lethal injection.

Some Christians believe that capital punishment is acceptable for the most serious crimes, such as murder. This punishment for the most serious crimes is recommended in the Old Testament. For example, Leviticus 24: 21 says: 'Whoever kills a man must be put to death.' Other Christians do not believe capital punishment is ever acceptable, because in their view all life is sacred and should be protected.

Bible bitz

If your brother sins, rebuke him, and if he repents, forgive him. If he sins against you seven times in a day, and seven times comes back to you and says, 'I repent,' forgive him.

Luke 17: 3 4

I will punish you as your deeds deserve, declares the Lord.

Jeremiah 21: 14

Submit yourselves for the Lord's sake to every authority instituted among men whether to the king ... or to governors, who are sent by him to punish those who do wrong.

I Peter 2: 13–14

Then the King [Jesus] will say to those on his right '... I was in prison and you came to visit me.' Then the righteous will answer him, 'Lord, when did we see you ... in prison and go to visit you?' The King will reply, 'I tell you the truth, whatever you did for one of the least of these brothers of mine, you did for me.'

Matthew 25: 34–40

Link it up

1 Copy out each Bible quote and explain what each of them suggests about the treatment of prisoners.

2 Try to link your explanations to the Christian teachings and the aims of punishment where appropriate.

Christian beliefs about and responses to the treatment of criminals

Christianity teaches forgiveness for wrongdoings. In the Bible, Jesus teaches his followers to forgive time and time again (Luke 17: 3–4). However, forgiveness does not mean that there should be no punishment for wrongdoing. Christians believe a criminal should pay for their crime, but any prison sentence should also provide the opportunity for the criminal to change and start afresh once they are released. Christians are commanded by Christ to care for the weak and prisoners (both victims and criminals) – treating each individual as if they were Christ himself.

The Catholic Church

In December 2004, the Catholic Bishops of England and Wales called for increased Christian understanding to be put into practice in the prison system. Their report specifically called for:

- a full working day of eight hours, five days a week, to help inmates acquire a WORK ETHIC and gain new skills
- more schemes to make the hiring of ex-offenders attractive to employers, for example skills training for specific jobs
- improved education in prisons
- more money for drugs treatment.

The Catholic Church teaches that punishment for crime should help the offenders to change their lives so that they can be integrated as valuable members of the community. The Church also believes that prisoners should have the right to vote. However, this is currently not allowed in the UK.

The Church of England

The Church of England also believes that offenders need to be prepared to return to society once they have served their punishment. The Church actively supports both victims of crime, criminals and the families of people in prison, for instance through the presence of prison CHAPLAINS. It also encourages its members to pray for the criminals and the justice system.

Restorative justice

Both the Catholic Church and the Church of England support the idea of RESTORATIVE JUSTICE. This allows the victim to choose to question the criminal and gain an insight into why they carried out the crime. In this form of justice, the criminal faces up to the harm that they have caused by meeting their victim. The idea is for them to make REPARATION for their crime. This means that through the conversations they have, the criminal seeks to repair some of the damage their crime has caused.

STRETCH
WHAT YOU KNOW

Desmond Tutu, the Archbishop of South Africa, said:

'I contend that there is another kind of justice, restorative justice…

'Here the central concern is not retribution or punishment but the healing of breaches, the redressing of imbalances, and the restoration of broken relationships. This kind of justice seeks to rehabilitate both the victim and the perpetrator, who should be given the opportunity to be reintegrated into the community he or she has injured by his or her offence. Thus we would claim that justice, restorative justice, is being served when efforts are made to work for healing, for forgiveness and for RECONCILIATION.'

1 What does restorative justice focus on?

2 How does restorative justice reflect the Bible quotes on page 89?

3 In what way do you think restorative justice can benefit society?

Case Study: *Elizabeth Fry*

Elizabeth Fry was a Quaker and one of the first people to insist that prisoners needed to be treated humanely. When Elizabeth Fry went to visit Newgate Prison in London in 1813, she discovered 300 women and their children, crammed together in two wards and two cells. Each woman had no more than a personal space of about 2m by 75cm.

Some of the women had already been convicted but others were still waiting to be tried. The prisoners slept on the floor without nightclothes or bedding and they all had to cook, wash and sleep in the same cell.

Following her first visit, Elizabeth Fry began to visit the women of the prison on a regular basis. She provided them with clothes and set up a school and a chapel in the prison. Later she introduced a system of supervision.

Elizabeth Fry campaigned for fairer treatment for all prisoners, including those who were sent to places such as Australia to serve their punishment. She firmly believed that capital punishment was not just wrong, but evil.

It was because of her faith and Christian values that she found the mistreatment of any human being unacceptable, as her faith and Christian values taught her. Fry's commitment to bringing about the humane treatment of prisoners, especially at Newgate, contributed to changing the prison system in the 1800s.

To discuss

3 Read the case study above. How did Elizabeth Fry's Christian faith influence her views and actions?

...HINTS

■ This question is asking you to link Christian beliefs/teachings to how criminals should be treated. So you could gives ideas on forgiveness and link these to Christian teachings.

■ Or you could refer to a specific Christian who has helped people in prison, such as Elizabeth Fry, giving details of her work and perhaps linking them to a Christian teaching such as the parable of the sheep and the goats – Matthew 25: 31–46. Remember do not narrate the parable itself but state what the meaning in the parable is.

■ Or you could refer to the aims of punishment (see page 88) and link these to Christian teachings. For instance, the aim of retribution links to the teaching in the Old Testament of 'an eye for an eye' (Exodus 21: 24).

EXAM FOCUS...

Explain Christian beliefs on the treatment of criminals.

question d), 6 marks

Christian beliefs about and responses to social injustice

Martin Luther King (1929–1968).

Mother Teresa (1910–1997).

Jackie Pullinger (1944–).

Desmond Tutu (1931–).

STRETCH
WHAT YOU KNOW

1 Pick one of the people from the photographs above.

2 Find out which group of people they stood up for and why.

3 Write a speech explaining why history must never forget such individuals, using the person you have researched as an example.

Each of the people in the photographs above has stood up for the weak or the oppressed. They are all Christians who believe or believed that injustices in society should not be left unchallenged. Another Christian who stood up for the oppressed was Oscar Romero (see page 92). Both he and Martin Luther King were assassinated for their views, even though they carried out all their protests in a non-violent manner.

Christian teachings

Christians believe in the value and DIGNITY of all human beings. This includes the weak, immigrants and other minority groups in society. Christians do not accept that one individual should possess fewer rights or values than another. For this reason all Christians are opposed to all forms of social injustice. Social injustice is a term used to describe situations where some people in society are given fewer rights and privileges than others. Christians believe that every human is equal in value in the eyes of God. In response to this belief, Christians aim to achieve justice for all people.

Bible bitz

When an alien lives with you in your land, do not ill treat him ... Love him as yourself, for you were aliens in Egypt.
Leviticus 19: 33–34

Do not take advantage of each other, but fear your God.
Leviticus 25: 17

Seek justice, encourage the oppressed. Defend the cause of the fatherless.
Isaiah 1: 17

The Spirit of the Lord is on me, because he has anointed me to preach good news to the poor. He has sent me to ... release the oppressed.
Luke 4: 18

Link it up

1 Explain what each Bible quote above means.

2 What evidence is there in these quotes to suggest that all people should be treated fairly?

Liberation theology

Liberation theology is the Christian idea that God has the power to change situations in the world that are unjust. Some Christians have taken this belief to mean that it is right to stand up against governments that oppress their people or to challenge abuses of power. As part of their commitment to liberation theology, Christians may take part in peaceful protests or actively take part in supporting those harmed by injustice, for example people who are imprisoned for political reasons and without a trial. Some supporters of liberation theology have been killed for speaking out against injustice. Among them was Oscar Romero.

Case Study: *Oscar Romero*

Oscar Romero became the Catholic Archbishop of El Salvador, in Central America, in 1977. At that time there was a great deal of social injustice in the country. A tiny, powerful and wealthy minority owned most of the land while the majority of the population were poor and oppressed.

Small Christian groups used to meet to worship and to seek comfort in the Bible for their situation in El Salvador. Each group had its own priest and an elected leader.

The landowners were worried that these groups might challenge their power and rights. The wealthy and powerful started campaigns against these groups. Some Christians were kidnapped, persecuted and murdered, vanishing without trace.

It was this kind of injustice that Romero spoke out against. He defended another priest, Father Grande, who had spoken out against the unfair treatment of 30,000 peasants in his own area. In 1977, Grande was murdered. Romero was sent to see his corpse in order to show him what happened to priests who challenged the powerful. However, rather than silence Romero, Grande's murder spurred him on to stand up for the poor and speak out more than ever before.

The government did not investigate Grande's death. The Sunday after the murder a Catholic MASS service was held in Romero's church. Thousands of Christians attended, united as one people who would not be put down. Romero asked the churches to record all the injustices that they observed, and these were passed on to the Pope. These actions brought Christians in El Salvador together and helped them to speak out against the oppression in their country.

In March 1980 Romero was shot, killed by a single bullet to the chest, which was fired from the back of his own church as he was performing Mass. Romero himself believed that murder did nothing to kill the work of God. His words and actions have continued through the work of others.

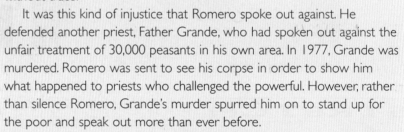

TASKS

1 Read the case study on Oscar Romero on page 92. Produce either a PowerPoint® presentation or a newspaper article to explain how Oscar Romero stood up against oppression in El Salvador and how this reflected his Christian beliefs.

2 You could carry out further research for this task by going to the CAFOD website.

To discuss

1 What kind of social injustice does Lorraine say she observed in Romania and how did she respond to it?

2 How else might a Christian respond to this type of injustice?

EXAM FOCUS...

Explain Christian response towards social injustice.

question d), 6 marks

Lorraine

In December 2001, my husband and I and a friend drove to Romania to deliver shoe boxes full of presents to orphans. I chose to go to Romania not just to take Christmas gifts to orphans, but also to show the children that they, as people, are of immense value. I was just one of a large number of people from around the world who cared about them and wanted to encourage them. I wanted them to see that God cares for each individual, even those whom the rest of society may reject.

Many of the orphans I visited still had living parents, but because of severe poverty they had been unable to care for their children and so had simply abandoned them. Many of these abandoned children had severe disabilities and had not been supported by the community they were born into. Orphanages and hospitals were in a state of disrepair, wards were old and damp and there was a complete lack of resources.

In contrast to this situation, the city, with its shops and festive lights, gave me the impression of a generally tolerant society. However, the disabled were treated as a different, lower class of citizen, and were stared at when we took them into the city for the first time.

As a Christian I believe that God made people in his image, and that he is able to give hope to all people. I felt the responsibility to share God's message of love, EQUALITY and hope with some of the rejected people I met in Romania. I will always remember their courage and determination, and the joy that simple gifts brought into their lives.

...HINTS

■ This question is asking you to state what a Christian would do and for you to state why linking your ideas to Christian beliefs/teachings.

■ You may wish to approach this question using specific Christian individuals who have devoted their lives to fighting injustice, giving examples of what they did and perhaps linking it to a Christian belief. For instance: Martin Luther King used peaceful protests in a bid to stop racism because he believed in 'turning the other cheek' (Matthew 5: 39).

■ You may wish to approach this question by using general ideas on how social injustice can be tackled but do remember to link these ideas to specific Christian teachings.

■ You may wish to explain Liberation Theology.

LET'S REVISE

Christian beliefs about the treatment of criminals

Christianity teaches forgiveness for wrongdoings.

The Catholic Church and Church of England support the idea of restorative justice.

Wrongdoing still has to be punished to pay for the damage done.

The Church of England often has chaplains in prisons to support the criminals and their families.

Christian beliefs about the treatment of criminals.

Prisoners should be given a chance to reform and start afresh on their release.

In 2004, the Catholic Church called for reform of prisons, including giving prisoners the right to vote.

Criminals and victims must both be cared for.

Jesus told his followers to care for both the weak and prisoners.

TASKS

1 Write a paragraph based on the diagram, taking into account each point and explaining it clearly.

2 Support as many points as possible with evidence or biblical references from your earlier work on this topic.

3 Create revision cards of your own for the topic 'Christianity, Peace and Justice'. For example on:
   - Christian attitudes towards war.
   - Christian attitudes towards violence and pacifism.
   - Christian responses to social injustice.

LET'S REvise

a) What is meant by 'social injustice'?   *1 mark*

  ▪ This is asking you to give a brief explanation of what is meant and so you could respond by saying 'unfair treatment of people' with perhaps an example to clarify your answer.

b) Give two examples of ways in which a Christian might respond to social injustice.   *2 marks*

  ▪ You could refer to the work of a specific Christian individual or you could give two general ways in which an individual might act, but remember to link these to Christian beliefs/teachings. Remember the question is asking for two examples.

c) How might a Christian respond to violence?   *3 marks*

  ▪ You would need to say what a Christian would do and why, linking the actions to biblical teachings.

d) Explain Christian attitudes to peace.   *6 marks*

  ▪ The keyword is 'attitudes' and so you could answer this question by either stating the reasons Christians believe in peace and how and why they would work for peace, or you could state that in some circumstances a Christian may have to resort to violence and explain why. Try and link the ideas to biblical teachings.

e) 'There can be no justice unless criminals are punished.'
Discuss this statement. You should include different, supported points of view and a personal viewpoint. You must refer to Christianity in your answer.   *12 marks*

  ▪ Remember – it is important to show different points of view and also your own personal point of view.
  ▪ This question is asking you to discuss and evaluate (look at the arguments for and against) and then come to a conclusion on whether the statement is true or false. You may not want to agree or disagree entirely – that is fine but you must support your conclusion with a valid reason.
  ▪ You will need to make sure you address the focus of the question so you will need to show that you understand what the word 'justice' means.
  ▪ You may wish to refer to the aims of punishment or the treatment of criminals in your answer, but make sure you link them to Christian beliefs/teachings.
  ▪ You could refer to the teachings on forgiveness or the second great commandment 'love your neighbour'.
  ▪ Remember to include your own personal view.

Christianity and Equality

Key Concepts

In this topic you will learn about:

- The biblical teaching about EQUALITY
- Christian attitudes towards other religions
- Christian attitudes towards faith
- Christian attitudes towards racism
- Christian attitudes towards gender
- Forgiveness and RECONCILIATION.

This topic is about Christian responses to moral issues related to equality. Christians believe in the equality of all humans. This belief affects their attitudes about prejudice in relation to race and gender. It also helps form their attitudes towards other religions. Alongside their belief in equality is also a strong belief in forgiveness and reconciliation with others.

Hot or not!

Self-esteem is about valuing yourself as a person. A person's self-esteem may be affected by the words or actions of those around them. In order to show respect to and value others it can help if a person is first able to see their own value and have a good sense of self-esteem.

Use Task 1 as a way to consider how words or actions may affect self-esteem.

To discuss

1 What causes people to value themselves?
2 Is it important that individuals value themselves? Explain your thoughts.

TASK

1 *Being called names*
   Being ignored
   Invited to join in
   Being thanked
   Treated differently to others
   Thoughtless comments
   Being valued

- Draw a thermometer like the one shown here.
- Place each of the above phrases on the thermometer based on how positive (hot) or how negative (cold) they make you feel about yourself.
- Think of two other phrases you would like to add that also affect your self-esteem.

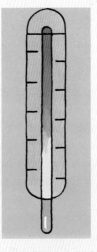

Who's Who

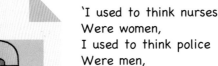

'I used to think nurses
Were women,
I used to think police
Were men,
I used to think poets
Were boring,
Until I became one of them.'

From 'Talking Turkeys,' Benjamin Zephaniah

TASKS

2 What do you think the 'Who's Who' poem is about?
3 How do you think our judgement of others can affect their self-esteem and sense of value?

Christian teachings

As we have seen already on page 30, Christians believe in the value and equality of all people. They believe that humans are created in God's image. This means that the perfect characteristics of God are reflected in all human beings, and for this reason they believe each individual has worth and value. This value is not dependent upon how others see us, or even what we think of ourselves. However, Christians do believe that each person should recognise their equal value to all others as God's unique creation, and also respect all other human beings, regardless of ethnicity, sex, age or religion, as equal to them.

To discuss

3 The 'Focus on London' information highlights some of the diversity found in the UK today. What can we do to show that diversity is valuable and that everyone is of equal value?

Focus on London

We now live in a diverse and delicately balanced society. This can be seen by looking at the range of people living in London alone.

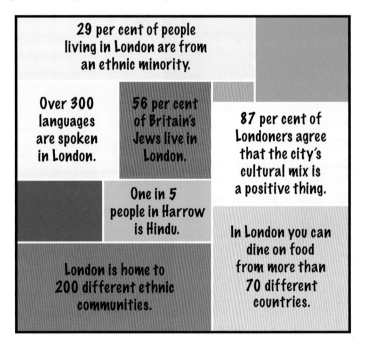

29 per cent of people living in London are from an ethnic minority.

Over 300 languages are spoken in London.

56 per cent of Britain's Jews live in London.

87 per cent of Londoners agree that the city's cultural mix is a positive thing.

One in 5 people in Harrow is Hindu.

In London you can dine on food from more than 70 different countries.

London is home to 200 different ethnic communities.

Diversity adds interest and value to our world. This patchwork of co-existing cultures and religions is something that many people in Christianity believe should be celebrated. Remember, Christians believe that each individual is unique, valuable and created by God.

TASKS

4 List the differences that can be observed between people in the world. Think beyond race and religion.

5 Create a collage of people, trying to incorporate as many differences as possible. Somewhere on your collage include one of the two following sentences, completed in your own words:

▥ All people are of equal value because …

or

▥ Celebrate diversity because …

The biblical teaching about equality

TASKS

1 Look at the collection of images. Explain how humans are diverse by giving examples from the images.

2 Now list all the things that humans have in common, beyond their physical existence.

The Bible teaches that God sees beyond ethnicity, gender, wealth, age, appearance, intellect, culture or ability and values all humans equally. No one is worth more or less to God.

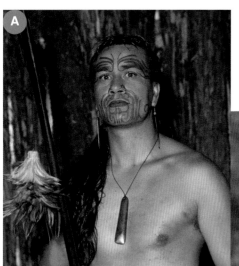

Maori man with facial tattoos.

Masai man with traditional jewellery.

Japanese woman in Tokyo, Japan.

Quechuan woman and daughter in Peru.

Scotsman in traditional kilt.

Bible bitz

There is neither Jew nor Greek, slave nor free, male nor female, for you are all one in Christ Jesus.

Galatians 3: 28

Then Peter began to speak: 'I now realise how true it is that God does not show favouritism but accepts men from every nation who fear him and do what is right.'

Acts 10: 34–35

My brothers, as believers in our glorious Lord Jesus Christ, don't show favouritism.

James 2: 1

For there is no difference between Jew and Gentile – the same Lord is Lord of all and richly blesses all who call on him.

Romans 10: 12

Love the Lord your God with all your heart and with all your soul and with all your strength and with all your mind... Love your neighbour as yourself.

Luke 10: 27

Link it up

Using the Bible quotes above, identify and list the ways they say humans should treat one another.

EXAM FOCUS...

Describe the biblical teachings on equality.

question d), 6 marks

The Bible also teaches that any person who prays to God will be listened to, and God will respond to all people in the way he knows is for the best. It instructs Christians to have the same attitude towards other people as God does – respecting and valuing them. The guiding rule when considering how to respond to another human being is to treat them in the way that you yourself would hope to be treated in their situation. Underpinning all of this is the belief that Christians should love God first and they will then be able to show their love to others through their words and actions.

the problem page

Dear Sarah,

For years at school I have had to deal with bullies who have called me names and made others stay away from me. I skived off school to stay away from them and have not done well in my GCSEs. I didn't tell anyone because I was embarrassed of what they'd called me and scared of what they'd do to me if I said anything. Now I have left school and I spend most of my time at home, my parents think I just haven't decided what I want to do next. I feel terrible about myself, I'm sure I look ugly and that people will hate me as soon as they see me. Help me! I want to go to college and do stuff normal people do but I can't because I feel such a waste of space.

TASK

3 Write a response to the problem page letter above that reflects the Christian teaching on human value. Use the Bible quotes on this page to help you complete your response.

...HINTS

■ This question is asking for 'teachings' so make sure you refer to them in your answer. However, do not just list them but try and explain them in your own words to show your understanding.

■ You do not have to know the biblical quotes exactly, but try to remember key words. For instance, when talking about God creating everyone the same, if you say that God created Adam and Eve '*in his image*' (Genesis 1: 27) the words '*in his image*' are enough to show the examiner what you are referring to.

The importance of inter-faith dialogue

TASK

4 ▥ Write down six statements about yourself. Two or three of the statements should be slightly untrue.
  ▥ Swap your set of statements with someone else in the class who doesn't know you very well.
  ▥ Now try to work out which of each other's statements are false. Do this without talking to each other.
  ▥ Compare what you have done. How accurate were you in selecting the false statements?
  ▥ Discuss how being allowed to talk to each other might have helped you to complete the task better.

To discuss

1 In what way could inter-faith dialogue be helpful in today's society?

In the task you should have identified how discussion with a partner would have helped you complete the activity more effectively. In all aspects of life, dialogue between people helps to increase our understanding of one another. Many Christians believe this is true both between different Christian DENOMINATIONS as well as between different religions.

Ecumenism

Each Christian denomination has its own set of beliefs, based on its own understanding of what the Bible says and how they interpret its teachings. There are therefore some beliefs that Christians may not agree upon – for example the authority of the Pope. However, some Christians believe that denominations ought to recognise that Christians are called to be one Church and that it is important to promote unity. This is known as ECUMENISM.

Inter-faith dialogue

Another dimension to ecumenism is INTER-FAITH DIALOGUE. Many Christians believe that discussion between faiths is a good and necessary way of appreciating one another's perspectives, recognising diversity and identifying commonly held values. This does not necessarily mean that they will agree with each other's beliefs or see them as right. These Christians believe that inter-faith dialogue is vital to help people to live together in peace, even though they have different beliefs.

Most Christians believe that their faith requires them to accept all people and to seek to live side by side with people of different faiths. Churches usually aim to develop good relationships with other religions, as well as to work with them as part of the global community whenever possible. Both the CHURCH OF ENGLAND and the CATHOLIC CHURCH employ people whose job it is to support the inter-faith relations.

Margaret

When I was a child in Dorset, I didn't know anyone who held a different faith from Christianity. I heard sermons about Christians working with people of other faiths, but there were no opportunities to get to know those people myself, and the Religious Education syllabus at my school in the 1960s did not cover any faiths other than Christianity. In my ignorance, I viewed people who belonged to other faiths warily, but with curiosity.

However, through my job as an RE teacher, I have loved meeting members of the Jewish community and local Muslims, getting to know them as friends, and understanding what their faith is and how it affects how they live.

Inter-faith dialogue is enormously important. There are beliefs and values which we share together, and there are also major differences we need to appreciate. Talking together is such an important way to build relationships, understand each other's way of life and why our differences matter. Dialogue means really trying to listen, being open to different ways of looking at life, and being willing to express what is important to us while respecting other people's right to disagree.

As a Christian, I believe that God's love is given for everyone and that, as a Christian, I have to find a way to show that love in all my words, actions and relationships. Inter-faith dialogue will always be demanding!

TASKS

Read Margaret's account.

5 What benefits from meeting people of different faiths does Margaret identify?

6 Margaret says that 'inter-faith dialogue will always be demanding'. What do you think she means by this?

STRETCH WHAT YOU KNOW

■ Taizé is an ecumenical centre in Burgundy, France. It is a place where Christians of different denominations can meet to pray and worship (see the website www.taize.fr/en).

■ The World Council of Churches is a crucial organisation in both the ecumenical and the inter-faith movement (see the website www.wcc-coe.org).

Using the internet, complete the following tasks for one or both of the organisations mentioned above:

1 When was the organisation established?

2 What is the purpose or aim of the organisation?

3 Provide one detailed example of the work the organisation does or the opportunities it provides for Christians around the world.

Christian attitudes towards other religions

While Christianity gives equal value to all humans, Christians may not agree with the beliefs others choose to hold, including the religions they may follow. Many Christians believe that when Jesus was crucified he took God's punishment for all human sin, providing a way for humans to be forgiven by God. God is able to forgive anyone who believes that Jesus' death happened as a way for them to have a connection with God. In this view, accepting Jesus as saviour is the only way God can be known. For this reason some Christians consider all other religions to be wrong.

Some Christians believe in EVANGELISM. They see it as their mission to share their faith with others. Sometimes these Christians become MISSIONARIES and decide to spend their lives encouraging others to become Christians. Missionaries may work in their own country or they may travel abroad to work as part of overseas mission teams.

One example of a MISSIONARY ORGANISATION is BMS World Mission. This organisation runs both short- and long-term missionary opportunities. Missionaries go abroad and carry out practical work as a way of sharing their faith and showing God's love – for example by going to Africa to work as a nurse in a missionary society hospital.

Other Christians believe that Christianity is only one way out of many to enter a relationship with God. They would not consider other religions to be wrong, but simply different. Christians who believe their faith is one of many routes to God may also share their beliefs with others. However, they are less likely to try to convince people to CONVERT to Christianity.

All Christians believe that, as individuals, people have to choose for themselves whether they want to enter the Christian faith. Another person cannot make that choice for them. For a Christian, faith is a relationship between the individual and God. People can simply share their own faith with others, making them aware of the possibility of such a relationship.

To discuss

I Do you think Christians should aim to share their faith with others? Why?

Volunteering abroad is increasingly popular among gap-year students.

(L to r) – Rabbi Shulamit Ambalu of the North London Central Synagogue, Omar Khalid of Finsbury Muslim Centre, Sikh Shivcharan Singh of the Guru Ramdas Centre and Halima Chergur of the North London Central Mosque in conversation at a memorial service for North London residents who died in the July 2005 blasts in London. The memorial was held on 22 September 2005 in the Union Chapel in Islington.

On 7 July 2005 there were four terrorist attacks in London. These caused over 700 injuries and the loss of 54 innocent lives. People from different religions and walks of life were affected.

TASKS

1 Identify the religions represented by their leaders in the photo.

2 Explain what message you think these leaders wanted to give to the nation by having a joint memorial service.

3 Explain what you think the benefits within a community might be of joint inter-faith acts. Do you think there are any negatives to such acts?

EXAM FOCUS...

'Everyone is entitled to their own view on religion, and no one should try to make you change your mind.'
Discuss this statement. You should include different, supported points of view and a personal viewpoint. You must refer to Christianity in your answer.

question e) 12 marks

...HINTS

■ Remember – it is important to show different points of view and also your own personal point of view.

■ This question is asking you to discuss and evaluate (look at the arguments for and against) and then come to a conclusion on whether the statement is true or false. You may not want to agree or disagree entirely – that is fine but you must support your conclusion with a valid reason.

■ You could answer this question by referring to the different Christian approaches to other religions, for example, some Christians believe that you have to be a Christian in order to get to heaven – link this to a specific Christian teaching. Whereas other Christians believe that if you lead a good life then God will accept you into heaven.

■ Remember to include your own personal viewpoint.

Christian attitudes towards racism

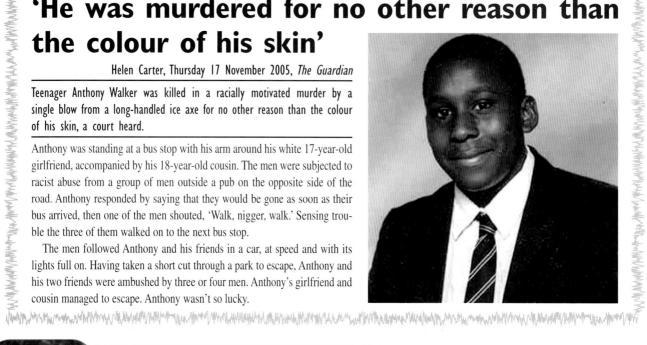

'He was murdered for no other reason than the colour of his skin'

Helen Carter, Thursday 17 November 2005, *The Guardian*

Teenager Anthony Walker was killed in a racially motivated murder by a single blow from a long-handled ice axe for no other reason than the colour of his skin, a court heard.

Anthony was standing at a bus stop with his arm around his white 17-year-old girlfriend, accompanied by his 18-year-old cousin. The men were subjected to racist abuse from a group of men outside a pub on the opposite side of the road. Anthony responded by saying that they would be gone as soon as their bus arrived, then one of the men shouted, 'Walk, nigger, walk.' Sensing trouble the three of them walked on to the next bus stop.

The men followed Anthony and his friends in a car, at speed and with its lights full on. Having taken a short cut through a park to escape, Anthony and his two friends were ambushed by three or four men. Anthony's girlfriend and cousin managed to escape. Anthony wasn't so lucky.

Chris

I found, and still find, this attack disturbingly graphic and utterly senseless. What could possess someone to inflict such unimaginable pain upon a fellow human being knowingly? As I read the articles and watched the news I felt overwhelmingly sad for, and angry at, the human race as a whole. This is what some of us have been reduced to and is what we are capable of. Killing an innocent A-Level student purely because of the colour of his skin. This illogical hatred or discrimination against someone simply because of their ethnicity or CREED is something I find both hard to comprehend and impossible to empathise with. Whilst being mainly about common MORAL VALUES, this view is reaffirmed by my Christian belief.

My faith in Christ helps to show me that discrimination on any scale, large or small, is wrong in the eyes of God. This Christian belief is constantly reiterated throughout the Bible. A relevant quote can be taken from the story of the Good Samaritan when Jesus tells the teacher of the law to 'Love your neighbour as you love yourself'. This shows us that God expects us all to treat one another as we wish to be treated ourselves, therefore not to discriminate against anyone. Aside from the extreme discrimination shown by these thoughtless men, the act of killing someone goes directly against most people's moral conscience, and certainly goes against all Christian teachings.

TASKS

1 How does Chris' response to Anthony Walker's murder reflect the biblical teaching on equality?

2 To what extent do you agree with Chris' response?

To discuss

Read the article above.

1 What attitude towards other individuals did the group of men and the murderer display?

2 What do you think society can do to challenge these attitudes?

Christian teachings

The biblical teaching on equality (see pages 98 and 99) guides Christian attitudes and responses towards any prejudice and discrimination, including racism. All denominations are united in their opposition to racism – an attitude which is often seen in their actions against it.

The Church of England

The Church of England teaches that God loves all people. In order for this message to be credible, it believes it must challenge racism. It does this through speaking out against racism through groups that are part of its Board for Social Responsibility. One such group is the Committee for Minority and Ethnic Anglican Concerns (CMEAC) – see the Case Study below.

Case Study: Committee for Minority and Ethnic Anglican Concerns

The Committee aims to encourage the involvement in the Church of its ethnic minority population. It aims to get rid of any racism within its community. The committee does many things, including:

- encouraging and enabling minority ethnic people who want to be ORDAINED or who want to be part of the LAY MINISTRY in the Church

- working together with other organisations committed to the wiping out of racism and supporting race awareness initiatives throughout society

- creating, ensuring and maintaining links with other faiths and cultures.

An example of the committee's work can be seen in a visit by a special working group in Nottingham in September 2005. The group spent time with members of the Rainbow Project, a church group that aims to develop relationships with people of other faiths and ethnic backgrounds. They also spent time in the city visiting other similar projects. After this visit the working group put together a report to recommend ways the DIOCESE could increase its membership from ethnic minority groups.

(from the Church of England website, www.cofe.anglican.org)

The Catholic Church

As early as 1537, the Catholic Church was speaking out against racism as seen in the form of the SLAVE TRADE. Catholics recognise the need to work to achieve unity between all people. The Catholic Association for Racial Justice wants the Church and society to 'value, respect and celebrate the equality and DIGNITY of all God's people' and it works in various ways to achieve this.

TASK

3 How does the work of CMEAC reflect the Christian attitude towards prejudice and discrimination?

STRETCH WHAT YOU KNOW

The Catholic Association for Racial Justice works in five main areas. These are:

- black and minority ethnic Catholics
- Catholic dioceses and PARISHES
- promotion of spiritual growth and development
- education
- advocacy work

1 Visit the association's website www.carj.co.uk to find out what work they do in each of these five areas.

2 Explain what effect you think the work of this organisation might have on the Church and on society in general.

The role of individuals in combating racism

The attitudes of Christians towards racism are also seen clearly in the lives of significant Christians in history. Such Christians include Martin Luther King, Trevor Huddleston and Archbishop Desmond Tutu.

Case Study: *Trevor Huddleston*

Trevor Huddleston was an ANGLICAN Bishop who believed that apartheid was evil and had to be destroyed. Apartheid was the official policy of racial segregation used in South Africa between 1948 and 1991. It involved political, legal and economic discrimination against non-whites. For example, non-whites were not allowed to vote, protest against injustice or have access to the same jobs as white people.

Trevor Huddleston lived and worked in South Africa from 1943 to 1956, in among the black communities, particularly in Soweto and Sophiatown.

He was involved in PROTESTS against apartheid. He believed that fighting apartheid was a battle against something deeply evil. He arrived at this belief through seeing how it affected the people he had responsibility for as a priest. He spoke out against the Christian Church worldwide and its lack of involvement in helping to bring an end to apartheid. He also took part in a call for a cultural BOYCOTT, asking international artists not to come to perform in South Africa,

because in doing so they were condoning apartheid. He also set up a protest group when plans were unveiled to remove all the 'black spots' from the white community where he was based.

He was invited to speak at many public meetings in England.

In 1960, he was appointed Bishop of Masasi in Southern Tanzania and, in 1978 Archbishop of Mauritius. However, his campaign against apartheid continued, and he became president of the anti-apartheid movement, based in Yorkshire in England. In this role he met the then Prime Minister Margaret Thatcher and advised that British SANCTIONS against South Africa would be a way of putting pressure on the government there and bringing an end to apartheid.

In the 1980s the system of apartheid gradually began to fall apart, and in 1994 the first completely free multiracial elections took place.

STRETCH WHAT YOU KNOW

Martin Luther King stood up against racism in America and was assassinated for his peaceful persistence to achieve equality for black people.

■ Find out about the key events in Martin Luther King's fight against prejudice in order to write an OBITUARY for him focusing on what he did and why he acted the way he did.

■ Ensure you make clear links between his Christian beliefs and his actions.

TASKS

4 Identify and list the ways in which Trevor Huddleston stood up against apartheid in South Africa.

5 How do Trevor Huddleston's actions reflect the Christian beliefs about equality and racism? Support your answer with reference to Christian teachings (see pages 99 and 105).

To discuss

3 ■ Compare the two images from South Africa taken during the time of apartheid.

■ What information do these two images provide that would challenge the Christian idea of equality?

■ Do you think similar contrasts exist in our world today?

Black housing in a South African township in the 1980s.

A white South African family outside their home in the mid-1980s.

EXAM FOCUS...

Explain Christian attitudes towards racism.

question d), 6 marks

...HINTS

■ The keyword in this question is 'attitudes' which mean that there are different approaches to the question.

■ You could refer to Christian teachings on equality, see page 97.

■ You could refer to the actions of certain Christian individuals that have been discussed in this topic but link their actions to Christian beliefs.

■ You could refer to the information relating to the teachings of the different Churches.

Christian attitudes towards gender

Christian teachings

Christianity is a religion that promotes equality. To many Christians this means that men and women should have equal rights to do the same jobs or take on the same roles if they are able to. Other Christians, however, believe that men and women have different roles in life, but that both roles are equally valuable. These Christians may, for example, believe that the role of the man is to provide for the family and that the role of the woman is primarily in the home and in caring for children.

In God's image
Christians believe in the equal worth of all humans; this includes the equal value of men and women. In Genesis 1: 27 both Adam and Eve were made in the image of God: men and women both have the character traits of God. In this section of the Bible it is clear to Christians that the physical differences between men and women are not important in terms of human value.

Woman as helper
In Genesis 2, Eve is created as a 'helper' for Adam. Some Christians interpret this to mean that women are to be subservient to men. However, the word 'helper' is translated from 'ezer' – a word also used in the Bible, to describe God (for example, in Deuteronomy 33: 29 where God is described as 'the helper' of Israel). Many Christians therefore believe it is unlikely that the word was used to represent woman as being less than a man.

Traditional roles
In the past, woman and men had very traditional roles in the family – man as breadwinner and woman as housewife – and these roles persist today in some families. Sometimes, the perception of a woman as wife and mother is seen as inferior to that of the man as the wage earner and head of the house. Proverbs 31 describes the ideal wife as being wise, strong and dignified, yet able to laugh. She is praised by her husband and children, who appreciate her hard work and commitment. Although as a wife and mother she takes on a uniquely feminine role, the woman is in no way shown to be of less value or of weaker character than the man. This is important to many Christians who believe that while men and women may take on separate roles their value and worth remain equal.

The role of women in the Bible
Women in the Bible are seen to fulfil a number of roles beyond the traditional ones of wife and mother. For example, in Judges 4: 4 the Bible speaks of Deborah as a prophetess and leader and in Judges 4: 21 Jael helps to get rid of the enemies of Israel. In Acts 18: 26 Priscilla is involved in teaching and in Romans 16 there are a number of women mentioned who were serving in the Church. Pliny The Younger, a Roman historian, also wrote about women in the Church who were MARTYRED for their faith (Letters 10: 96–97).

TASKS
1 What view do most Christians have of the value of men and women?
2 In Genesis 2 God creates Eve as a 'helper'. What are the different ways that this term is understood by Christians?
3 Which biblical teachings support the Christian view that sexism is wrong?
4 Explain whether you think it is possible for men and women to have different roles and yet still be valued as equals.

To discuss

Read the article 'Women "lose out" in top jobs race'.

1 What do you think Nicola Brewer meant when she said 'We always speak of a glass ceiling. These figures reveal that in some cases it appears to be made of reinforced concrete'?

2 What are some of the reasons given for women underachieving in the workplace?

3 What do you think could be done to change this trend?

4 Read the Christian teachings opposite. How do you think Christians would respond to this article?

Jesus' treatment of women

Jesus himself challenged many cultural stereotypes by the way he treated women. In biblical times women were certainly treated with less respect and value than men, but Jesus gave them respect. For example, in John 4: 9 when Jesus met a Samaritan woman at the well he spoke with her, which was not usual practice at the time; even the disciples were surprised. In the same way that Jesus accepted this woman as worth taking time out to talk to, Christians believe God has time for men and women alike and so should everyone.

All one in Christ

Paul sums up the biblical teaching on all matters of prejudice when he writes 'There is neither Jew nor Greek, there is neither slave nor free man, there is neither male nor female; for you are all one in Christ Jesus' (Galatians 3: 28). Christians aim to treat all people with the love of God. God's love is not determined by what gender someone is and in the same way Christians believe that their treatment of people should also not be affected by gender.

Women 'lose out' in top jobs race

The number of women holding senior posts in politics, the law and the media has fallen compared with last year, according to a report.

(http://news.bbc.co.uk)

The Equality and Human Rights Commission (EHRC) said that in twelve of 25 job categories it studied, there were fewer women holding top posts.

Women's representation had increased in eight areas, including company directors and the civil service.

The EHRC said its annual study of women in top positions of power and influence across public and private sectors showed the biggest number of reversals since the report was started five years ago.

Nicola Brewer, the chief executive of the EHRC, said: 'We always speak of a glass ceiling. These figures reveal that in some cases it appears to be made of reinforced concrete.'

The commission said opportunities for ambitious women to reach the top of their career were changing at a 'snail's pace'.

It blamed Britain's business culture of long working days and inflexible working practices for discouraging women who want to both work and raise a family.

Miss Brewer told BBC Radio 4's *Today* programme: 'There is a bit of discrimination still going on and that still needs to be challenged. At the commission's helpline, we still get a high proportion of calls from women at work who are pregnant who are suffering difficulties.

'There are also bigger things going on about how the workplace is organised, how it's really quite inflexible, how there is a lot of occupational segregation and how the definition of success is still quite old-fashioned.'

'Draining combination'

The report, Sex and Power, said: 'Often women experience a draining combination of outdated working practices and a long hours culture alongside the absence of appropriate high quality, affordable child care or social care.'

Rebekah Brooks was one of the few women at the top of her career when she was editor of the *Sun* newspaper.

The role of women in Christian society

TASKS

a 'Equality is about giving the same value to all people.'

b 'Equality is about everyone having the same opportunities and roles.'

1 Explain which statement is illustrated by the scales picture.

2 Which statement, a or b, best reflects your own view on what equality is?

3 From what you have studied so far, which statement do you think best illustrates the Christian view?

In the picture above, balance on the scales is achieved. Even though the weights are made up in different ways, the two sides of the scales are of equal value. In the same way some people believe that equality between people does not necessarily mean being identical to one another in every way. In fact, it is about being valued equally while perhaps having different roles in life. This approach to equality is reflected to some extent within the Christian Church.

Christian Churches

In the Church of England women may now be ordained to be VICARS, taking on the role of preaching and PASTORAL CARE in a diocese. They are, however, still not permitted to become bishops.

Many other denominations, such as the main FREE CHURCHES (Methodist, Baptist, United Reformed and Salvation Army), also allow both men and women to become ministers. This reflects their interpretation of the equality of all people as expressed in the Bible.

In the Catholic Church women are not allowed to be ordained and so cannot become priests. The Catholic Church believes this for a variety of reasons, including:

- the fact that God chose to come to Earth as a man
- that all Jesus' disciples were men
- that Jesus chose Peter to be the head of the Church.

However, women are a valued part of the Catholic Church and its community, and often work in the Church in other ways, for example as Eucharistic ministers (people who give out the bread and wine which have been consecrated by a priest, who visit the sick, etc.).

An Anglican female vicar. The first group of 1000 women was ordained in 1994.

Roman Catholic priests gathered in Cologne, Germany, for Pope Benedict XVI's Mass for the 20th Youth Day celebrations on 21 August 2005.

EXAM FOCUS...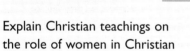

Explain Christian teachings on the role of women in Christian society.

question d), 6 marks

TASKS

4 How do the two photos reflect the contrast between the Catholic and the Church of England's views on the role of women in the Church?
5 Explain how equality is shown in each denomination's view on the role of women in the Church.
6 Explain what role you think women should play in the life of a Church. Use the Christian teachings on page 108 and Bible quotes (see page 23) to support your answer.

...HINTS

■ This question is asking you to explain 'teachings' so make sure you say what a woman is allowed to do in the Church and in everyday life and link the idea to a Christian viewpoint – either a Bible teaching or a Church teaching.
■ You could refer to the roles of women in the different churches using the points of view of both the Church of England and the Catholic Church.
■ You could refer to the working woman or the role of a woman as a mother, but remember to link the idea to a biblical or Church teaching.
■ You can refer to the teachings on page 108 to help you.

Forgiveness and reconciliation

To discuss

By the end of 2005, there had been more than 1800 murders in Northern Ireland after 30 years of unresolved conflict.

In June 2004, Chief Constable Hugh Orde talked of the need for a reconciliation process.

1 Read the article on this page. How do you think the law about Northern Irish fugitives was meant to support the process of reconciliation?

2 Do you think the law represents a good way of bringing about reconciliation?

3 From your knowledge of Christianity how do you think Christians may have reacted to this law?

4 Read the quote below. What link do you think Desmond Tutu is making between the future and forgiveness?

5 How does the Christian belief in forgiveness help to build relationships with God and people?

'Without forgiveness, there is no future.'

Archbishop Desmond Tutu, Nobel Peace Prize winner (1931–)

The Future for Northern Ireland Fugitives

MPs have voted to allow PARAMILITARY FUGITIVES to return to Northern Ireland without having to be imprisoned for their crimes, including acts of murder. This will apply to around 150 people who carried out crimes before 1998.

Many of those affected by the terrorists' crimes are deeply unhappy with this decision.

The families of four murdered Royal Ulster Constabulary police officers expressed their opposition to the proposed law by lobbying the prime minister.

Under the new law, fugitives would go to a special tribunal to have their cases heard. If a fugitive was then found guilty they would be freed without having to go to jail.

Christian teachings

Christians believe that God is merciful, and that once he forgives sins he remembers them no more. Christians believe that God forgives those who REPENT. This means they are sorry for what they have done and that they intend to change and not repeat the same mistake in the future. However, Christians believe that humans will continually make mistakes because they are not perfect, and God in his perfection will continue to forgive people who are truly sorry for their actions.

God reconciled himself to people through the sacrifice of his son Jesus on the cross, and his forgiveness of humans is possible because of Jesus' death and RESURRECTION. Through the EUCHARIST in the Anglican Church or MASS in the Catholic Church, Christians can remember and receive God's forgiveness through the celebration of Christ's sacrifice.

Christians believe that, in response to God's love and forgiveness of people, they should try to show the same attitude to those around them. Forgiveness from one human to another should not be limited. Christians believe that people must forgive others and rebuild relationships every time a person is truly sorry for something they have done wrong, whatever this may be.

The Catholic Church

In the Catholic Church a person can attend confession to receive God's forgiveness. During this time a priest will hear an individual's confessions in a small cubicle divided in two, with a grille to speak through. Whatever a priest hears during this time is confidential. The priest acts on behalf of God to lead the confessor to PENITENCE and forgiveness. A priest may advise a person to say certain prayers or to correct the thing that they did wrong.

BB Bible bitz

Forgive us our sins, for we also forgive everyone who sins against us.

Luke 11: 4

Love your enemies and pray for those who persecute you.

Matthew 5: 44

Be kind and compassionate to one another, forgiving each other, just as in Christ God forgave you.

Ephesians 4: 32

Forgive, and you will be forgiven.

Luke 6: 37

If we confess our sins, he [God] is faithful and just and will forgive us our sins.

I John 1: 9

If your brother sins, rebuke him, and if he repents, forgive him.

Luke 17: 3

Link it up

1 Identify from the Bible quotes above what a Christians needs to achieve to receive forgiveness.
2 Forgiveness from God is closely linked to a person's willingness to forgive others, including their enemies. How do you think this might affect the way a Christian behaves in their relationships with others?

EXAM FOCUS...

Explain how Christians' beliefs about forgiveness and reconciliation may affect the way they treat others.

question d), 6 marks

Case Study: *An interview with the mother of murdered teenager Anthony Walker (see page 104)*

Anthony Walker's devastated mother Gee said she will forgive his killers – but only when they show genuine remorse.

Sitting in the family church and clutching the hand of Anthony's sister, 20-year-old Dominique, she wept as she explained the void his death has created.

'We'll never get over this. Someone has taken a piece of my heart. How do you mend a broken heart? You can't mend a broken heart.'

Despite her obvious pain, Mrs Walker's strong Christian faith means she cannot hate Barton and Taylor [Anthony's murderers]. She said: 'I can't hate. I brought up my children in this church to love. I teach them to love, to respect themselves and respect others. Hatred is a life sentence. What does bitterness do? It eats you up inside like a cancer. We don't want to serve a life sentence with those people.'

Asked if she can forgive the killers, Mrs Walker replied: 'We just hope these lads find it in their hearts to forgive themselves, once they realise what they have done and they accept it.

'I've not seen remorse yet. They must accept what they did before they can forgive themselves. If they are not remorseful, it is pointless. If they came to me and apologised, I would tell them.'

Asked if Anthony would forgive them, she replied: 'Yes. That's all I can say. Without a doubt, he would have forgiven them, because that was Anthony.'

(Press Association)

TASKS

1 Why do you think Gee Walker places such importance on the need for Anthony's killers to be remorseful before she can forgive them?
2 How does her understanding of forgiveness reflect Christian beliefs? You could refer to some biblical quotes in your answer.

...HINTS

- This question is asking you to link Christian beliefs/teachings to actions. So you will need to say what a Christian would do and why: 'They would do ... because ...'.
- You could refer to the Lord's prayer in which Christians ask God to forgive them their sins as long as they forgive others (Luke 11: 4).
- You could refer to the teachings of Jesus such as 'forgive seventy times seven' (Matthew 18: 22).
- You need to refer to both forgiveness and reconciliation so make sure you understand what the words mean.
- You could refer to the actions of a specific Christian individual such as Mrs Walker (see above).

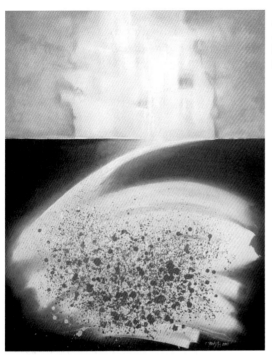

Redemption by Monsma – Christ sacrificed his life's blood to set us free.

An offering to our Lord by Sans Lumier – Christians must rest at the foot of the cross.

Redemption, by Hinz fine art – Jesus died on the cross to redeem humankind from its sins.

TASKS

3 In what way do the images above encourage people to think about forgiveness and reconciliation?

4 Design a piece of art that would help someone to meditate on the need to forgive and rebuild a relationship that has been broken.

LET'S **RE**VISE

Christian attitudes towards other religions

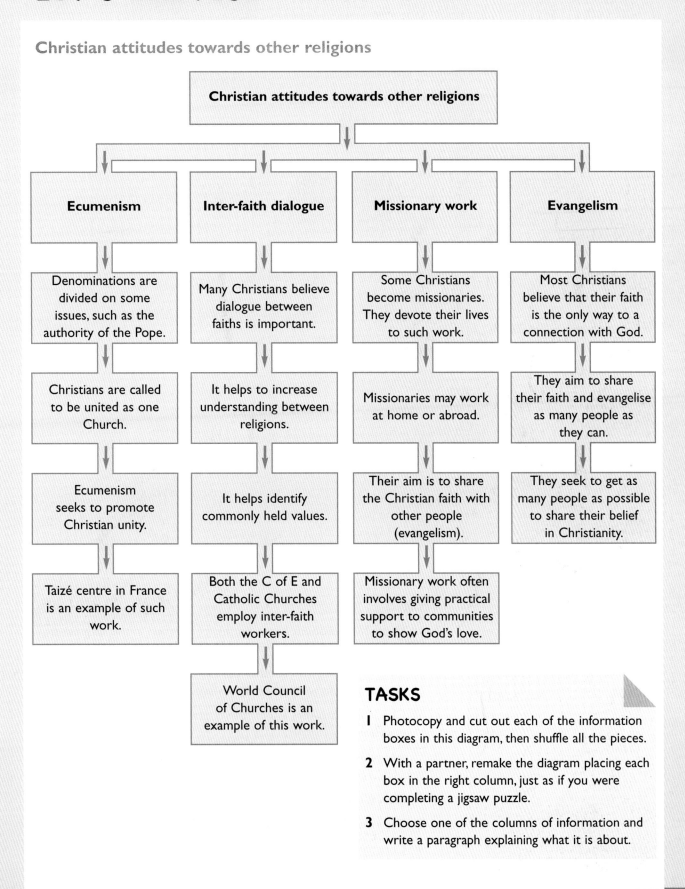

Christian attitudes towards other religions

Ecumenism	Inter-faith dialogue	Missionary work	Evangelism
Denominations are divided on some issues, such as the authority of the Pope.	Many Christians believe dialogue between faiths is important.	Some Christians become missionaries. They devote their lives to such work.	Most Christians believe that their faith is the only way to a connection with God.
Christians are called to be united as one Church.	It helps to increase understanding between religions.	Missionaries may work at home or abroad.	They aim to share their faith and evangelise as many people as they can.
Ecumenism seeks to promote Christian unity.	It helps identify commonly held values.	Their aim is to share the Christian faith with other people (evangelism).	They seek to get as many people as possible to share their belief in Christianity.
Taizé centre in France is an example of such work.	Both the C of E and Catholic Churches employ inter-faith workers.	Missionary work often involves giving practical support to communities to show God's love.	
	World Council of Churches is an example of this work.		

TASKS

1 Photocopy and cut out each of the information boxes in this diagram, then shuffle all the pieces.

2 With a partner, remake the diagram placing each box in the right column, just as if you were completing a jigsaw puzzle.

3 Choose one of the columns of information and write a paragraph explaining what it is about.

LET'S **RE**VISE

Christian attitudes towards racism

Individuals: Martin
Luther King,
Trevor Huddleston

Organisations: The Anglican
Committee for Minority and
Ethnic Anglican Concerns

Churches recognise the need to educate
people against racism.

Christians do not tolerate racism and will try to oppose it.

The Christian teaching on the equality of all people regardless of race is the
foundation for all their attitudes towards racism.

TASKS

1 ▨ Write five questions based on the information in this diagram that
    would test someone's knowledge of this section.

  ▨ Swap questions with another person in the class and answer their
    questions from what you have revised.

  ▨ Check your answers against the diagram and correct them as
    necessary.

2 Create revision cards of your own for the topic 'Christianity and
    equality'. For example:

  ▨ Biblical teaching about equality.

  ▨ The role of women in Christian society.

  ▨ Christian beliefs about forgiveness and reconciliation.

LET'S REvise

a) What is meant by reconciliation? *1 mark*

- This question is asking for a simple explanation of the word so you could say 'mending bridges' or 'making friends again' or 'the ending of fighting'.

b) Give two examples of racist behaviour. *2 marks*

- You could refer to either apartheid or the segregation laws in America which Martin Luther King Junior fought against, or you could refer to examples of racism which have been reported in the news.

c) Describe Christian beliefs about other religions. *3 marks*

- You could show the different views held by Christians about other religions and link them to a teaching.

d) Explain Christian teachings about equality. *6 marks*

- The keyword in this question is 'teachings'. So you could use teachings from both the Old and the New Testaments. See page 99 to help you.
- Remember that you must not just make a list of the teachings/quotes but that you need to explain them in your own words to show your understanding of what they mean and how they relate to the question.

e) 'Women should stay at home while the men go out to work.'
Discuss this statement. You should include different, supported points of view and a personal viewpoint. You must refer to Christianity in your answer. *12 marks*

- Remember – it is important to show different points of view and also your own personal point of view.
- This question is asking you to discuss and evaluate (look at the arguments for and against) and then come to a conclusion on whether the statement is true or false. You may not want to agree or disagree entirely – that is fine but you must support your conclusion with a valid reason.
- Try not to get carried away and just include your personal opinion of sexism – your opinion is needed but the answer also requires a Christian perspective. Give the different Christian views on the role of women and link them to Christian teachings/beliefs.

Christianity and the Media

In this topic you will learn about:

- The different forms of media and their influence
- The portrayal of Christianity and important religious figures in the media
- Responses and attitudes towards films, books and comics which focus on religious or philosophical messages
- The way Christianity uses the media
- Censorship and freedom of speech
- Beliefs and attitudes towards the portrayal of sex and violence.

The media are the different means of communication in society such as newspapers, magazines, television, radio and the internet. These sometimes include portrayals of Christianity and religious figures which can cause controversy if the image presented is thought to be inaccurate, offensive or too narrow by some believers. In the media there is a constant balance being sought between avoiding using material that may cause offence to some people, including Christians, and allowing freedom of speech which is a basic human right. However, Christianity also makes use of the media to represent itself to Christians and non-Christians and to educate them. Christians have their own beliefs and attitudes towards the portrayal of sex and violence in the media, particularly if they are not portrayed in a way that reflects or supports the teaching of the Bible.

The different forms of media and their influence

To discuss

1 Look at and read the facts below about the various forms of media. What can you say about the role of the media in society based on this information?

68 per cent of 8–18 year olds have a TV in their bedroom; 54 per cent have a DVD/VCR player and 37 per cent have cable/satellite TV. In 63 per cent of households, the TV is 'usually' on during meals.

In 1993 Talk Radio became the first e-radio site, providing radio via the internet. Among the hundreds of radio stations available in the UK there are some that are only digital or available via satellite, for example UCB radio. So to listen to these stations you need a DAB radio, internet access or satellite TV.

One of the earliest UK daily national newspapers was *The Times*. It built its reputation through featuring important people from the areas of politics, science, literature and art. The top-selling UK newspaper in 2008 was the *News of the World*. It focuses on celebrity stories and populist news articles.

Broadband users spend 48 per cent of their leisure time surfing the internet.

Over the past 300 years the media have grown, developed and adapted. Now people have the possibility of instant access to immediate news and information directly into their own homes via the internet. E-mailing and texting are often more popular than making a phone call, while search engines and social networking sites influence a large number of people as they prioritise the results to any given search.

Advertising is present in most of the media and is just one of the ways in which the media can influence people's thoughts, attitudes and choices. Advertising aims to persuade people to purchase or use particular products and brands. In 2007 Apple increased the amount it spent on advertising itunes.com in the US by 279 per cent in the same year they also released their iPhone. This example reflects the importance placed on advertising and its effects by companies who make their money through successful selling.

The media can have a great deal of influence over the lives of individuals in other ways. For example, in 1938 in America there was a radio broadcast of the novel *War of the Worlds* and some people who listened believed that an actual Martian space invasion was taking place and fled their homes in a state of panic.

The media can also be used to influence people through PROPAGANDA. For example, in the 1930s and 1940s the Nazis used radio broadcasts, posters, books and films to create anti-Semitism. One such film was *The Eternal Jew*. The film was made like a documentary and throughout it depicted Jews as being wandering PARASITES. Propaganda such as this helped create an environment where the HOLOCAUST could take place.

More recently some critics have blamed violent computer games and films for aggressive behaviour in society. Others believe that the media can be influential in creating stereotypes and prejudices, as described in the articles on this page.

Islam and the Western Media:

Stereotypes and misconceptions about Islam in the media are rooted in prejudice, and ignorance, says Bassil Akel, a Muslim writer

Islam is the fastest growing religion in the west. Nevertheless, the west has many stereotypes and misconceptions about Islam that are due to the media, prejudice, and ignorance. Islam is often looked on as an 'extremist', 'terrorist' or 'fundamental' religion. Many people hate Islam and do not want to acknowledge its true teachings. In many cases, the media's reports about Islam are incorrect due to ignorance. This is one of the reasons why the west often hates Islam. In contrast to what many westerners think of Islam, Islam is a peaceful religion, which does not promote any forms of uncalled for fighting or 'terrorist' actions.

www.islamfortoday.com

Survey: Christians Face Discrimination

CBN News. 19 March 2007

One in three British Christians say they've experienced discrimination in the media, the workplace and their communities.

The results came from a BBC survey.

The London *Evening Standard* reports that there's growing concern among British Christians that their faith is being marginalised by multiculturalism.

A minister with a Christian campaigning group blames, 'an aggressive SECULARIST agenda' for some of the changes in his country.

www.cbn.com

To discuss

2 Can you think of ways in which the media has had a positive influence on people's perception of Christianity?

TASKS

Read the two internet articles above.

1 What are the similarities between each article?
2 To what extent do you think the claims in each are true? Use your own experience of the media to support your view.

The portrayal of Christianity and important religious figures in the media

Christianity in the news

The media in the UK often reports on religious responses to significant news events. An example of this was in 2003 when the CATHOLIC CHURCH and the CHURCH OF ENGLAND issued a joint statement to the press about their concerns over the morality of invading Iraq.

The media also reports on events that impact on the Christian Church. For example:

- In 2005 the press reported on the inauguration MASS of Pope Benedict XVI when he called for Christian unity.
- In 2007 Churches were reported in the media as supporting the government's plans for increasing the numbers of faith schools.
- In 2008 the media reported on the disagreements within the Church of England about ordaining women bishops and homosexual ministers.

Often the Church's responses to moral issues make headline news as they may be contrary to popular secular belief. For example, in 2001 the BBC reported Pope John Paul II referring to genetic research using human EMBRYOS as evil as he warned President Bush of the USA against it.

The news coverage of Christianity portrays a complex image. It shows that in many ways Christianity is united on major world issues while at the same time Churches are divided within themselves over matters of faith and belief, suggesting any unity is fragile. While the Christian beliefs and attitudes given in media reports may be counter to those in society on topical issues, it does show that the Church has a response and that it is engaged with society.

Christianity on TV

Often Christianity is represented by a church minister in soaps, comedy and light entertainment programmes. For example, Ashley in *Emmerdale* (1996 onwards) and more controversially Father Kieron, the gay priest on *Hollyoaks* (2008). Probably the most famous portrayal of a VICAR in entertainment is *The Vicar of Dibley*. In this comedy many stereotypes about the religion are confronted. First and most obviously is the fact that the vicar is female but there are also stereotypes about the type of community that the Church serves by focusing on the old or the eccentric. The comedy relies largely on the portrayal of the church community as naïve, incompetent and out of touch. They do, however, unite behind their vicar and work together as a community. Another commonly recognised Christian character is Dot Cotton from *Eastenders* who regularly quotes Bible passages to people in response to their behaviour or questions; she has been involved in storylines involving crime and euthanasia.

A marriage from *The Vicar of Dibley*. Alice, the verger, marries Hugo, the son of a local landowner.

Religious Programmes – God-slots embrace the spirit of the age

The Independent, 22 May 2006.
Sally Turner

Attracting audiences to religious programmes has always been a challenge. But an injection of reality television seems to be providing the answer. Sally Turner reports

In May of 2006, an episode of BBC2's religious 'reality' series *The Monastery* beat ITV's *Celebrity Love Island* in the ratings. Having pushed the boundaries with food, sex, and sport, it was only a matter of time before producers gave faith the reality treatment as well.

The Convent followed four women from different walks of life as they spent six weeks with a closed community of nuns. It's an approach that appeals to society's obsession with the make-over; instead of plastic surgery and home improvements we're being sold the possibility of spiritual transformation.

When the 2006 Religious Television Awards were held at Lambeth Palace, the official home of the Archbishop of Canterbury, three of the shortlisted shows for the *Radio Times*-sponsored Audience Award were reality shows. With church attendances in decline, programme-makers face the same challenge as the religious establishment – how to make faith entertaining, progressive and accessible.

The shortlisted reality shows – *The Monastery*, *Priest Idol* and the observational documentary series *A Seaside Parish* – all relied on the human interest angle. If religion is going to engage a new generation it needs to entertain.

www.religionnewsblog.com/14738/

ITV accused of 'abandoning religious TV'

The Guardian, 22 May 2008.
Maggie Brown

ITV was attacked yesterday for entering just three religious programmes for the annual Sandford St Martin Trust's awards rewarding excellence in the genre.

The Reverend Colin Morris, the chair of the awards judges and a former head of BBC religious broadcasting, speaking at the prize ceremony at Lambeth Palace in London, said he thought it was sad that ITV seemed to have 'abandoned religious broadcasting'.

ITV put three programmes up for this year's Sandford St Martin Trust awards, out of a total of 43 submissions from broadcast-

ers. BBC2 documentary *The Boys from Baghdad High* won the trust's award.

Conservative MP Ann Widdecombe, who presented the awards, also commented on the entries: 'There is a great deal about the body on television, cookery, beauty, exercise, and psycho babble, but very little about the soul.'

Widdecombe also pointed to the fact that three of the four programmes to win awards were about Islamic themes and society. 'I hope next year the winners will come from the Christian religion. There is a creeping embarrassment about Christianity,' she said.

TASKS

1 Read both of the newspaper articles.

2 Explain why you think the reality programme *The Monastery* was so successful in the Religious Television Awards of 2006.

3 Give reasons for why you think ITV produced fewer religious programmes in 2008.

4 Do you agree there is a 'creeping embarrassment about Christianity' in the media? Give reasons.

Important religious figures in the media

Christian leaders are often interviewed by the media in relation to Church or current world affairs. For example:

- In February 2008 the Archbishop of Canterbury, Rowan Williams, was interviewed on the radio programme *The World at One* following a controversial speech in which he commented about Muslim law in Britain. One suggestion he gave was that Muslims should be able to deal with marriage breakdowns using their own law rather than the British divorce.
- In March 2008 the Archbishop of Westminster, Cardinal Cormac Murphy-O'Connor, was interviewed about his call for political parties to let politicians vote how they wanted (rather than how their party told them) on the bill that would allow human DNA to be mixed with an animal egg that has had its nucleus removed. The embryo would then be used for medical research for up to fourteen days before it was destroyed.

At times Christian leaders also appear on panels debating current issues. For example, in February 2008 the Right Reverend Stephen Lowe, the Bishop of Hulme and the Church of England's first bishop for urban life and faith, appeared on the BBC's *Question Time* programme to discuss current issues of the day. Christian leaders can also be the subject of newspaper cartoons which seek to make a point through the use of humour. The media does not avoid referring to Christian leaders in this way.

To discuss

1 In what way is the cartoon below meant to be humorous?
2 What does the cartoon suggest about the unity of the Church at this time on the issue of homosexual rights?
3 Do you think it is acceptable to depict Church leaders in cartoons in this way?

This cartoon by Steve Bell appeared in October 2003 in *The Guardian* when Anglicans were meeting and discussing the rights of homosexuals.

Desmond Tutu speaking at the Tibetan freedom torch rally vigil in San Francisco, USA on 8 April 2008. Tutu was also in the news in July 2008 when he said he would support the use of United Nations forces in Zimbabwe to help deal with the humanitarian crisis in the country.

Rowan Williams, the Archbishop of Canterbury, has appeared in the media when speaking out about poverty, for expressing concern about the number of children receiving custodial sentences, for speaking about shariah (Islamic) law in Britain, and for the row in the Church of England over homosexuality.

Pope Benedict II received media coverage in 2008 when he visited the USA and spoke to the United Nations, urging them to work together to solve world crises. In July 2008 the Pope was again in the media, this time because he was apologising for child abuse carried out by some Catholic priests.

EXAM FOCUS...

Describe Christian attitudes towards the way Christianity has been portrayed in the media.
question d), 6 marks

...HINTS

▪ The keyword in this question is 'attitudes' so this means that there are different Christian responses: some may approve and some may disapprove.
▪ So you will need to give some positive examples of how Christianity has been shown in the media (remember this can be television, newspapers, the internet, etc.) and some negative examples.
▪ You can use examples of how specific Christian individuals have been shown or the religion itself.

To discuss

4 List the various ways in which each of the three Christian leaders on this page have appeared in the media.

5 Do you know of any other ways any of these three Christian leaders have appeared in the media and how they were portrayed? If you have access to the internet do a search on each leader on the BBC news website: http://news.bbc.co.uk.

6 Based on the information you have gathered in 4 and 5 above, discuss the following statements in groups and decide which you believe to be correct or incorrect:

▪ Christian leaders are often portrayed as having a role to play in world issues.
▪ Christian leaders are portrayed as defenders of their own denomination.
▪ The portrayal of Christian leaders by the media suggests that they don't have a role to play in modern society.
▪ Christian leaders are always held up as perfect role models by the media.

7 Add a statement of your own which you think is correct about the media's portrayal of Christian leaders.

Look at the photos and the captions below and answer the questions:

1 Do you think writers like Dan Brown or film makers have any responsibility to remain true to Christian beliefs when using the religion for entertainment? Explain your answer.

2 Mel Gibson's film *The Passion of the Christ* aimed to show the death of Christ in as real a way as possible, sticking to the biblical account of the events:

a) Why do you think he wanted to produce Jesus' death in such a violently graphic way?

b) Why do you think the violence in his film has been so controversial when there are many films that include such violence?

Responses and attitudes towards films, books and comics that focus on religious or philosophical messages

There are a number of films, books and comics which aim to retell all or part of the Bible. Examples of this include *The Passion of the Christ*, a film produced by Mel Gibson, *The Cockney Bible* by Mike Coles and various comic forms of the Bible. At other times fictional stories are created that include elements of biblical truth that are then built upon; this is true of the book *The Da Vinci Code* by Dan Brown.

Christian responses to such types of media vary. Some are offended by the graphic nature of the content or the misrepresentation of their faith. Other Christians appreciate the realism found in films like *The Passion of the Christ*. For many Christians new adapted versions of the Bible that may increase its reading audience are seen as a positive thing.

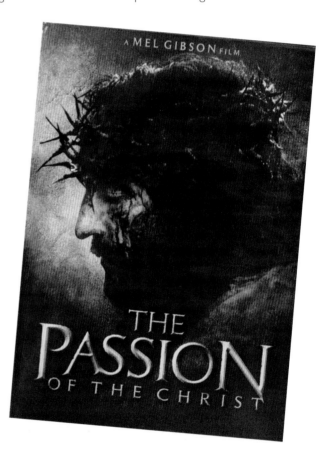

US magazine *Entertainment Weekly* claimed that Mel Gibson's film *The Passion of the Christ* was the most controversial film to date in 2003. Mel Gibson is a highly committed Catholic and was aiming to create a true-to-scripture film of the final hours of the life of Christ. However, the cause of the controversy was the graphic nature of the violence in the film coupled with what some believe to be the highly anti-Semitic content.

The film based on the book, *The Da Vinci Code*, by Dan Brown reached number 13 in the most controversial films list in 2003. The book and, subsequently, the film claimed that Jesus Christ had a relationship and children with Mary Magdalene.

Simon

Perhaps I should first explain why I feel it is important for Christians to participate in debate regarding films. I consider cinema to be the modern equivalent of parables – with the potential to spread a good or bad message. To deny the power of storytelling to my mind is foolish at best, given that Jesus himself used parables to expound on his message. I think the reason he did so is because, as powerful as any sermon may be, a personal story (either true or fictitious) can have far greater power. Three excellent films from last year – Hotel Rwanda, Lord of War and The Constant Gardener – enabled me to connect emotionally with the problems facing Africa far more than any number of Live 8s. And after watching About Schmidt, the first thing I did was sponsor a child!

Every Christian who feels led to engage with culture in the way I do will need to develop their own code of conduct to decide what they are and aren't happy to expose themselves to. Given that Basic Instinct 2 was likely to contain strong pornographic imagery, I chose not to see it, as exposure to such material could potentially be a stumbling block for my thought life … It will not be the same for every Christian, and I am sure others have different thresholds to me for what they will and won't watch in good conscience before God.

Simon Dillon is a Christian movie reviewer on http://uk.god.tv

To discuss

1 How does Simon believe that films can be seen as similar to the parables of Jesus?

2 Simon says that the story in a film can be more powerful than a sermon. What examples does he give to support this view?

3 Discuss examples of films that have had a positive effect on your attitude or behaviour.

4 On what grounds does Simon suggest that the use of violence in a film may be considered justifiable?

5 What do you think Simon means when he says 'I am sure others have different thresholds to me for what they will and won't watch in good conscience before God'?

Use the examples from the *Comic Book Bible* and *The Bible in Cockney* to help you complete the tasks.

3 Turn the story from *The Bible in Cockney* into a comic strip.

4 Read the Lord's Prayer below and then write it in your own style of Cockney rhyming slang.

5 How effective do you think it is to use comic strips to tell Bible stories?

6 Do you think producing the Bible in these ways is of any benefit? Give reasons.

7 Why do some Christians not like the Bible being translated into street language or cockney rhyming slang?

The Lord's Prayer

He said to them, "When you pray, say:
'Father,
  hallowed be your name,
    your kingdom come.
  Give us each day our daily bread.
  Forgive us our sins,
      for we also forgive everyone
      who sins against us.
    And lead us not into
  temptation.'"

(Luke 11: 2–4)

Books and comics

The Bible can be quite difficult for some people to understand as the language used in older translations such as the King James Bible (1611) may not be familiar to today's readers. In order to make it more accessible to the current generation different versions of the Bible have been created. For example, Christian author Rob Lacey published a copy called the *Street Bible* (2003) in which he uses street language – he uses phrases such as 'God's PA system' when Jesus hears God speak from heaven. In 2001 teacher Mike Coles turned much of the Bible into Cockney rhyming slang to make it more interesting for his pupils from London's East End. The former Archbishop of Canterbury, Dr George Carey, approved of this translation; he said it put energy and passion back into the stories. Other Christians believe that such translations water down the original manuscripts too much and so the teaching lacks clarity and is not as reliable. They may also believe that these translations lack respect for God's word and undermine its rightful authority.

Christians often use pictures when telling Bible stories to children and there are many illustrated versions of the Bible. Another way the Bible has been published is in comic form. Children and young people are often more attracted to comics than to text-only books and it is usually fairly easy to tell what the story is about through the pictures in comics. Comics also enable the use of humour to help communicate a message. However, Christians do not use comic versions of the Bible for study as they lack depth but they do help bring the Bible to an appropriate level for children who may then want to go on and read the Bible for themselves as they get older. Most Christians believe that anything that encourages more people to read the Bible is a good thing.

The Comic Book Bible by Rob Suggs.

The Bible in Cockney by Mike Coles.

Jesus heals some geezer
(Matthew 8: 1–4, Luke 5: 12–16)

There was this geezer who had leprosy (some dodgy skin disease), and he came to Jesus, fell on his biscuits and said, 'If you want to, please make me clean.'

Jesus felt really sorry for the geezer. He stretched out his Ramsgate and touched the geezer, Jesus said, 'Be clean.'

Well would you Adam and Eve it, the disease left the geezer immediately and he was clean.

Jesus then said quite seriously to him as he sent him on his way, 'Now don't tell anyone about this, will ya? Go straight to the priest and he'll check you out, and then make sure you offer up a little sacrifice that Moses rabbit and porked about and that'll prove to all the people that you're clean.

But the geezer was so happy, he started to tell people everywhere what had happened. In fact, he rabbit and porked about it so much that Jesus couldn't go into town publicly. He 'ad to stay out in the country, and people came to see him from all over the place.

EXAM FOCUS...

Explain how a Christian might respond to books written about Christianity.

question d), 6 marks

...HINTS

- This question is asking you to give ideas on how a Christian would react, either positively or negatively, to books written about Christianity. So you will need to give examples and explain whether the reaction would be good or bad.

- You could refer to the Bible and the different versions.

- You could refer to controversial books such as *The Da Vinci Code*.

- You could refer to children's stories from the Bible.

The way Christianity uses the media

Bible bitz

He said to them, 'Go into all the world and preach the good news to all creation.'

Mark 16: 15

Coming to his hometown, he began teaching the people in their synagogue, and they were amazed. 'Where did this man get this wisdom and these miraculous powers?' they asked.

Matthew 13: 54

Day after day, in the temple courts and from house to house, they (the Apostles) never stopped teaching and proclaiming the good news that Jesus is the Christ.

Acts 5: 42

The church sent them (Paul and Barnabas) on their way, and as they travelled through Phoenicia and Samaria, they told how the Gentiles had been converted. This news made all the brothers very glad.

Acts 15: 3

Therefore go and make disciples of all nations, baptising them in the name of the Father and of the Son and of the Holy Spirit.

Matthew 28: 19

Television

If you flick through the channels on digital television it isn't long before you come across *The God Channel*, *The Gospel Channel* and *Faith* among other Christian broadcasting channels. The same is true of digital radio with stations such as United Christian Broadcasters and Premier Christian Radio. These channels and stations have two aims, first to encourage those people who are not Christians to be convinced of the truth of Christianity and so CONVERT to the faith and secondly to teach people about Christianity through biblical teaching. This broadcasting can include Christian music, sermons and interviews with Christians.

An example of a Christian programme on terrestrial television is *Songs of Praise*. *Songs of Praise* gives those who cannot attend church the possibility of engaging in similar worship in their own home. The programme includes singing as well as interviews with Christians in various Christian communities around the country. For many this programme may act as a source of encouragement for them in their Christian life. For others the programme simply gives them a snapshot of what Christian worship and belief may be like.

The internet

Many Christian Churches and organisations now have dedicated websites in order to reach a wider audience. These websites often have pages for spiritual help, including opportunities for people to become Christians or for Christians to get support with their faith.

One example is the Billy Graham Evangelistic Association website (www.billygraham.org). This organisation aims to convert people to Christianity and to bring preaching from the Bible to an international congregation. The website has a section giving spiritual help and it includes a short video on how to achieve peace with God. The website also provides links to their radio ministries and opportunities to subscribe to their magazines which inform people about their work and include biblical teaching.

Another example is The Damaris Trust's website. The Damaris Trust is an educational charity with a Christian foundation. It works with people of all faiths and those with none. It aims to relate biblical Christian faith to contemporary popular culture. Damaris operates in three areas – church, school and media. Damaris Media is an example of Christians using the media to educate. It explores contemporary issues and compares popular ideas with biblical teaching using a range of media including videos and podcasts. Opposite is a screenshot from their website which shows the range of media they use.

TASKS

1 Read through the information from the Damaris Media webpage.

2 List the different types of media the Damaris Trust uses and what it uses each type for.

3 Do you think the Damaris approach of using a range of media would make Christian education more or less effective? Explain your answer.

Home page of the Damaris Media website which is a part of the Damaris Trust (www.damaris.org).

Link it up

1 Which Bible quotes on page 128 indicate that Christians should:
   a) educate others about their faith
   b) aim to see people converted to Christianity?

2 Describe how Christianity uses the media to do these two things.

3 Explain why you think Christians are using the media as a tool to do this.

EXAM FOCUS...

Explain Christian attitudes towards the use of the media for education.

question d), 6 marks

...HINTS

■ The keyword in this question is 'attitudes'. You are being asked to give different Christian responses to using different forms of media, such as television, books, internet, etc. with the aim of educating/teaching people about the Christian religion.

■ You may wish to approach this question by giving examples which might show a negative or positive attitude, such as the EVANGELICAL programmes shown on the television.

■ You may wish to approach the question by showing how the media could be used to 'spread the good news', and link this idea to specific Christian teachings.

Censorship and freedom of speech

TASKS

1 Explain what is meant by the terms censorship and freedom of speech.
2 What is one of the exceptions to the right to the freedom of speech when talking about religion?
3 Explain how important you think this exception is.
4 The recommendation to decriminalise blasphemy said 'religious groups must tolerate ... critical public statements and debate about their activities, teachings and beliefs.' In what way can criticism and public debate be a useful process?
5 What do you think may be the effects of open and free discussion about Christianity and other religions? You may find it helpful to divide your page into two columns and write the good effects on one side and any negative effects on the other.

Censorship

Censorship is when a government or authority looks at and decides to suppress or change print or broadcast media because it is considered to be harmful, sensitive or objectionable in some way. Religious censorship is when any material objectionable to a certain faith is removed.

In the UK and Europe people are free to express their views about any religion unless the content is likely to incite violence or discrimination against its followers. However, until October 2007 blasphemy was a criminal offence under European law. Decriminalisation was recommended because 'religious groups must tolerate, as must other groups, critical public statements and debate about their activities, teachings and beliefs.'

The UK followed suit and on 8 July 2008 its law against blasphemy was also abolished. The Archbishops of Canterbury and York both said that in the right conditions the Church of England would support this change in law providing it was not seen as a licence to attack or insult religious beliefs and believers. This change in the law firmly supports the freedom of speech.

Freedom of speech

Freedom of speech is being able to speak freely without censorship or fear of punishment. The right to freedom of speech is recognised as a human right in Article 19 of the UNIVERSAL DECLARATION OF HUMAN RIGHTS. This right includes: 'freedom to hold opinions without interference and to seek, receive and impart information and ideas through any media and regardless of frontiers.'

Attitudes and responses to issues raised by freedom of speech

The right to the freedom of speech obviously allows Christians to express freely their own faith and beliefs even though these are not the beliefs of many other people in society. Christians want to share their faith and believe that they are called to witness it to the world, therefore the right to freedom of speech for Christians is highly valued. In parts of the world where such freedom is not available many Christians face punishment for still continuing to speak out about their faith.

However, the same right that gives such freedom to Christians also allows their own beliefs to be criticised and challenged by others. At times Christians may feel that freedom of speech has been allowed to go too far and that the mockery of their faith in some broadcasts is unacceptable. *Jerry Springer – The Opera* was one such broadcast that created a strong reaction from Christians who believed that the show was deliberately offensive and unacceptable. In the same way the Muslim community reacted in outrage over the publication in Denmark of cartoons depicting the prophet Muhammad. In this case the BBC reported on the issues surrounding the cartoons but refused to publish them. These examples raise the issue as to the boundaries, if any, that there should be over freedom of speech in the media.

To discuss

Read the news article about *Jerry Springer – The Opera* and discuss the three questions raised at the end of the article.

Should the BBC have shown Jerry Springer opera?

BBC.co.uk, 17 January 2005

A Christian prayer group, Christian Voice, will bring a private blasphemy prosecution against the BBC after the screening of *Jerry Springer – The Opera* on Saturday.

The show depicted American talk show host Jerry Springer meeting transsexuals and a troupe of tap-dancing Ku Klux Klansmen.

The BBC has defended its decision, saying that as a public service broadcaster it should provide programmes that appeal to the differing tastes and interests of people in the UK.

Do you think *Jerry Springer – The Opera* should have been broadcast by the BBC? Is Christian Voice right to object? Is the BBC's justification valid?

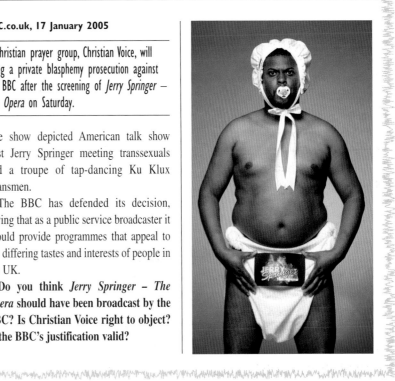

TASKS

6 Was the BBC right to not show any of the cartoons that had caused offence to Muslims? Give reasons.

7 Do you think that by allowing the Jerry Springer opera, which offended some Christians, but by not showing the cartoons of Muhammad, because they offended Muslims, the BBC were making a distinction between what is acceptable for Christianity compared to Islam? Give reasons.

In 2006 cartoons were printed in Danish newspapers which satirised (mocked) the Muslim prophet Muhammad. This caused great offence to Muslims who do not believe that he should be pictured in any way. Around the world there were violent Muslim PROTESTS as a result of the drawings. In the UK the BBC chose to report on the issue but did not show any of the cartoons. Some viewers believed the BBC were spineless for choosing not to show them as it would cause offence to Muslims in the UK. One viewer wrote: 'It appears that you are scared of the reaction from Muslims, while you were not concerned about offending Christians when you screened *Jerry Springer – The Opera*. This is a case of double standards.'

More recently, in 2008, the film *The Golden Compass* caused large-scale Christian protests in America. This film was a dramatisation of the first book in *His Dark Materials* trilogy by Philip Pullman. The film failed to do well in the USA as there were BOYCOTTS of it by so many Christians. This is because they thought that the film, like the book, contained many subtly suggested challenges to Catholicism.

Members of Christian organisations burn copies of TV licences outside BBC Television Centre in London, 7 January 2005, in protest at the decision by the BBC to transmit *Jerry Springer – The Opera*. The broadcaster received more than 20,000 complaints after it revealed it would air the show.

TASKS

8 **a)** Explain how the Christian protesters against *The Golden Compass* in America have exercised their right to free speech.

b) In this example what is the possible outcome of the Christian use of free speech?

9 Describe some of the effects that having the freedom of speech leads to.

10 What do you think should be the limitations, if any, on freedom of speech? Give reasons.

The Golden Compass was based on the first book in *His Dark Materials* trilogy written by Philip Pullman. The trilogy is a reworking of the story of the Garden of Eden and the Fall of Man.

STRETCH WHAT YOU KNOW

In China, during the cultural revolution between 1966 and 1976, every church in China was closed down as the government was completely against the practice of any religion. Today in China religion is still tightly controlled by the communist government. There have been a number of reported arrests of Catholic leaders, particularly in the Hebei Province in the northern area of China. Writing on the national review website (www.nationalreview.com) David Aikman, a journalist, reported on the challenges faced by Christians in China. One such example in the public eye is Timothy Sui, a conductor. Aikman wrote: 'For three years Su has conducted first-class orchestras and choirs in public performances in Beijing of Handel's Messiah in Chinese. He was permitted to conduct one performance in Guangzhou, but local authorities in Shanghai and other cities cancelled the performances. Su is highly respected as a musician, and he is publicly known to be a Christian, a fact that has caused him problems when it comes to more performances of Christian worship music.'

1 Explain how the censorship in China is affecting the work of Timothy Su.
2 Knowing the opposition that they are likely to be faced with why do you think Christians in China are still prepared to speak out and live out their faith?
3 Compare the freedom of speech enjoyed by Christians in the UK with the restrictive practices in China.
4 Using your work from this chapter explain the importance of the freedom of speech and whether this should be balanced with any level of censorship.

EXAM FOCUS...

'People should never be allowed to make fun of Christianity in the media.'
Discuss this statement. You should include different, supported points of view and a personal viewpoint. You must refer to Christianity in your answer.

question e), 12 marks

...HINTS

- Remember – it is important to show different points of view and also your own personal point of view.

- This question is asking you to discuss and evaluate (look at the arguments for and against) and then come to a conclusion on whether the statement is true or false. You may not want to agree or disagree entirely – that is fine but you must support your conclusion with a valid reason.

- You will need to approach this question with the use of many different examples showing that some Christians may take offence at some of the ways in which Christianity is portrayed in the media whilst others may see it as harmless fun.

- You could use examples of *Jerry Springer – The Opera* as mentioned in this topic, or you could refer to *Father Ted* or the *The Vicar of Dibley*.

- You could refer to the freedom of speech laws.

- Remember to include your own opinion and support it with the use of examples.

Beliefs and attitudes towards the portrayal of sex and violence

Some Christians choose to not watch TV or films in order to avoid seeing things which are unacceptable to them and which may then remain in their thoughts or affect their actions in a negative way. A biblical example of this is when King David spent time watching a married woman as she bathed, and he later committed ADULTERY and murder as a result.

James

Sex

Big brother, pop videos, teen magazines, movies; we live in a culture that is obsessed with sex. Sex is used in all kinds of ways by the media, especially to get people to buy things; for example the Lynx effect adverts which claim if you wear their deodorant then you'll be magically turned into an irresistible hunk.

The media's view of sex is if it feels good, do it, as long as you are not hurting anyone; in other words, have sex as much as you can, with whoever you can, but do it safely.

As a Christian I believe God invented sex and that he invented it as a great thing, in fact there's a whole book in the Bible called Song of Songs, which is a guy and a girl telling each other how much they fancy each other!

I also believe that God gave us instructions on how we can enjoy life (and sex) the most, and these instructions are found in the Bible. The Bible says that the place for sex is in marriage, between two people who have made a public commitment to each other. This is where sex belongs and is at its most enjoyable.

Violence

You can't turn on your TV without seeing something to do with violence. The news often is about wars, shootings or stabbings and reports the sadness and devastation caused by this violence.

However there is another side to violence in the media. There are many movies which portray violence as being cool, and glamorise the 'gangster' lifestyle. The same could be said of some video games; a lot of them are based around how many people you can either beat up or shoot. Whilst there is an element of fun to these things, as a Christian I am concerned about the effects these have on the people who watch/play them.

As a Christian I am looking forward to heaven; the Bible says in a book called Revelation that in heaven there will be no more death, mourning, crying or pain, in other words there will be no violence, and no more sadness and devastation caused by violence.

TASKS

1 How does James compare the message of sex in the media with what he believes to be the Christian attitude towards sex?

2 James says that he is concerned about the effects that violence in films and games may have on people. What do you think he means by this?

3 Do you think the 'fun' element of violence when used in film or games outweighs any negative impact that it may have on people? Give reasons.

The use of sex and violence in programmes and films is often contrary to Christian teaching. For example, Christianity teaches that sex should not be part of a casual relationship as it is considered a gift from God that brings together two people as one flesh once they are married, and that violence should be avoided as Jesus urges his followers to turn the other cheek and to love their enemy. For this reason some Christians believe that programmes that show casual sex or violence are evil and directly opposed to the will of God – such media is therefore unacceptable to them.

Other Christians have a different view. Dr Edward McNulty, a minister from New York and editor of a magazine called *Visual Parables*, which explores religious themes in secular movies, said: 'Life has a lot of R- and X-rated factors in it, but we don't run away from it; we engage it.' By this he means that sex and violence are part of life, and film or TV simply tell stories about life, real or fictional and so they inevitably include these things. However, Christians who agree with this are not suggesting that sex and violence should be glorified or centralised in programmes but that sometimes these form a legitimate part of the story. Christians may see film and TV as stories through which they can find truths about God in the same way that Jesus used parables to help his listeners understand God. For example, the parable of the Good Samaritan contains violence.

All Christians are wary of films that simply sensationalise either sex or violence. They believe that sex is a gift from God and excessive unprovoked violence is in no way justifiable. Portrayal of sex or violence in these ways is unacceptable to them. Crusader Entertainment is a Christian film company that only produces films with a universal or parental guidance rating; Bob Coton, its marketing director, described the film *The Omega Code* which entered the US box office charts at No 10 in 2003: 'We believe that gratuitous violence, use of drugs or smoking, sex and profanity will obscure the positive message we wish to impart. Tens of millions of people will pay to see positive films with Christian values.'

To discuss

1 What attitude does Bob Coton seem to have towards the portrayal of sex and violence in film?

2 To what extent do you agree with Bob Coton's claim that gratuitous violence and sex obscure any positive message in a film?

3 If 'tens of millions of people will pay to see positive films with Christian values' why do you think there are so few of these films in the cinemas today?

EXAM FOCUS...

Explain Christian attitudes towards the portrayal of sex and violence in the media.
question d), 6 marks

...HINTS

■ The keyword in this question is 'attitudes' which means that Christians will have different responses to how sex and violence are shown in the media.

■ You will need to refer to both aspects, 'sex' and 'violence', in your answer and try and link the different responses to specific Christian teachings. For example, you could say that some Christians are against all the sex scenes shown on television because they believe sex is a gift from God and should only be used in marriage yet the scenes on television do not reflect this view. You could then link this statement to the teaching of Paul that the body is a temple (1 Corinthians 6: 19).

LET'S **RE**VISE

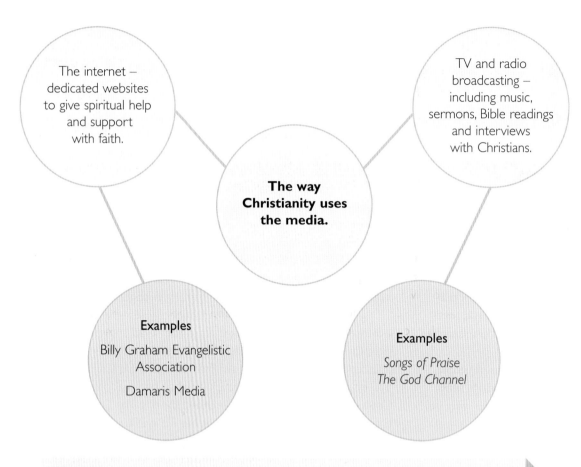

The internet – dedicated websites to give spiritual help and support with faith.

TV and radio broadcasting – including music, sermons, Bible readings and interviews with Christians.

The way Christianity uses the media.

Examples

Billy Graham Evangelistic Association

Damaris Media

Examples

Songs of Praise
The God Channel

TASKS

1 Write two paragraphs based on the content of the circles (one for TV and radio and one for the internet). Include Bible quotes in your paragraphs to show how the use of the media is fulfilling the teaching in the Bible about educating and converting people to Christianity.

2 Write a review of a recent film you have seen or book that you have read from a Christian perspective. Include:
▦ how appropriate the use of violence and sex was
▦ whether there was a Christian moral message that could be gained from it.

If you have not got a film or book that you could review you could always review an advert. For example James (page 134) refers to the Lynx deodorant adverts.

3 Create revision cards of your own for the topic 'Christianity and the Media'. For example on:
▦ The portrayal of Christianity and important religious figures in the media.
▦ Responses and attitudes towards films, books and comics which focus on religious or philosophical messages.
▦ Censorship and freedom of speech.
▦ Beliefs and attitudes towards the portrayal of sex and violence.

LET'S REVISE

a) What is meant by 'censorship'? *1 mark*

▓ You will need to give a brief explanation of 'censorship'. You could perhaps state that it is when people in authority stop people saying what they want.

b) Give two examples of how Christians can use the media to spread the Christian message. *2 marks*

▓ Make sure you give two examples. You could refer to the internet, specific programmes on TV such as *Songs of Praise*, billboards outside churches, or information leaflets or books.

c) Describe Christian attitudes towards the portrayal of important Christians in the media. *3 marks*

▓ The keyword in this question is 'attitudes' so you can respond to this question by showing examples of how some Christian leaders are portrayed in the media (you can use any types of media you like) either negatively or positively.

▓ You could refer to leaders such as the Pope or the Archbishop of Canterbury or specific Christian individuals who are believed to be good role models such as Desmond Tutu, Mother Teresa, etc.

d) Explain Christian attitudes towards films about stories from the Bible. *6 marks*

▓ The keyword in this question is 'attitudes' so you can show both negative and positive examples of how Christians have reacted to specific films.

▓ The other keyword is 'films' – so make sure your examples are of films and not books or anything else.

▓ You could refer to Mel Gibson's film *The Passions of the Christ*, or older films such as *The Ten Commandments* or *The Greatest Story Ever Told* (starring Charlton Heston), or even children's cartoon films such as *The Miracle Maker*.

▓ You could refer to *The Da Vinci Code* being a film which to some Christians has made a mockery of the story of Jesus.

e) 'Only Christians should be involved in the making of Christian programmes or films.'
Discuss this statement. You should include different, supported points of view and a personal viewpoint. You must refer to Christianity in your answer. *12 marks*

▓ Remember – it is important to show different points of view and also your own personal point of view.

▓ This question is asking you to discuss and evaluate (look at the arguments for and against) and then come to a conclusion on whether the statement is true or false. You may not want to agree or disagree entirely – that is fine but you must support your conclusion with a valid reason.

▓ You will need to use specific examples to support your ideas, showing why it might be important that only Christians could present the true Christian views/beliefs or why it might be important that an unbiased point of view should be used.

▓ You could refer to examples such as documentary programmes shown on television or you could refer to the films you may have already mentioned in part d) of this question.

▓ Remember to include your own personal viewpoint.

Glossary

Abstinence   Refraining from something. In this context, choosing not to have sex.

Adultery   Having sex with someone other than your spouse when married, or having sex as an unmarried person with someone who is married.

Anglicans   Members of the Church of England.

Anti-vivisection   Against animal testing. This includes being against using animals for medical research.

Boycotts   Challenges against something or someone by refusing to have any relation with them. This may be a country refusing to trade with another or an individual or group choosing not to buy or use a product.

CAFOD   The Catholic Agency For Overseas Development. The organisation raises funds from the Catholic community in England and Wales to promote development around the world.

Catholic Church   Historically the oldest branch of the Christian Church, it has its spiritual centre in the Vatican, Rome, and is led by the Pope.

Celibate   Remaining unmarried and choosing not to have sexual intercourse.

Chaplain   A minister. The term is used particularly for Christian ministers in the army, navy and air force.

Church of England   The Church founded by Henry VIII in the early sixteenth century.

Cohabitation   Living together as husband and wife without actually being married.

Compassion   An expression of care and concern for those in need.

Conceive   To create an embryo by a man's sperm penetrating a woman's egg starting a pregnancy.

Conception   The point at which an embryo is created.

Conscientious objector   A person who refuses to fight in a war or to enrol in the army because they believe that weapons and fighting are wrong.

Contraception   Natural or artificial means to reduce the likelihood of a pregnancy occurring as a result of sex.

Convert   To change someone's belief or religion, for example, from Islam to Christianity.

Creed   A statement of beliefs.

Denominations   The different types of Churches within Christianity that have different forms of leadership, worship and doctrines.

Developed nations   The wealthiest countries in the world, including England and the USA.

Developing nations   The poorest countries in the world, including most African and South American countries.

Dignity   A sense of respect and value.

Diocese   A geographical area under the jurisdiction of a bishop.

Double effect   The argument that actions such as euthanasia can be allowed if they are a side-effect of a good action such as pain relief.

Embryo   The first collection of cells that develops in the womb when a woman becomes pregnant.

Ecumenism   The sense of universal belonging and togetherness of the entire Christian Church.

Equality   The condition of being of the same value and importance as something or someone else.

Eucharist   The sacrament in the Christian Church when bread and wine are received to symbolise the body and blood of Jesus.

Evangelical   Christians who believe that they should convert others to the Christian faith.

Foetus   The growing baby in the womb.

Fornication   Sexual relations occurring outside of marriage.

Free Churches   Non-conformist Churches that are free from state control, including the Methodist, Baptist and United Reformed Church.

General Synod   The national assembly of the Church of England. It has the power to amend Church teachings.

Holocaust   Generally used to describe the genocide of approximately six million European Jews during the Second World War by the Nazis under the leadership of Adolf Hitler.

Hospices   Places where terminally ill people can go for respite and nursing care.

Hydration   Providing water for the body.

Infertile   Said of someone unable to conceive naturally. For a woman, this occurs because she does not ovulate (produce eggs). A man is infertile if he does not produce healthy sperm.

Inter-faith dialogue   On-going debate and relations between different faiths and communities, for example between Christians, Muslims and Jews.

Lay ministry   The volunteer ministry, made up of church-goers, that supports ordained ministers.

Living will   A legal document declaring a person's wish to die a natural death. This may involve stopping or not giving treatment in certain situations.

Martyr   A person who voluntarily suffers death as the penalty for proclaiming their religion and refusing to deny it.

Mass   The Catholic Church's name for Eucharist.

Missionaries   Evangelical people who travel to other countries to spread their faith.

Missionary organisation   Organisation set up to do missionary work.

Moral values   The set of values a person has about what is right or wrong.

Obituary   An account of a person's life written after they have died.

One World Week   An international movement led by people organising local events to celebrate being part of one diverse world, and raise awareness about and act on issues of global justice.

Oppressed   Said of people being overpowered and ruled by others unfairly.

Ordained   Appointed, through a Christian ceremony, to a ministerial role within the Church.

Paramilitary fugitive   A member of a civilian military organisation running away from the law. The fugitive may be wanted for either questioning or arrest for an illegal act.

Parasite   An organism living in, with, or on another organism.

Parish   The area that a church minister or priest is responsible for in the Church of England.

Pastoral care   A minister's work in looking after the personal, physical, spiritual and social well-being of an individual or group.

Penitence   Feeling sorry for a wrongdoing and making amends for it through positive action.

Persecute   To mistreat and discriminate against an individual or a group through time.

Persistent vegetative state   A condition in which patients with severe brain damage have progressed from a state of coma to a state of 'wakefulness without awareness'.

Pharmaceutical research   Research carried out for the purpose of developing new medicines.

Poverty line   The level of income below which a person cannot afford to buy what they need to live.

Pro-choice   Believing that a woman has the right to choose whether to go ahead with a pregnancy or not, on the basis of her circumstances.

Pro-life   Opposed to abortion and believing that all human life should be protected, even before birth.

Propaganda   The spreading of information to deliberately further a cause or to damage an opposing cause.

Protests   A declaration of dissent against something or someone. A protest can be spoken, written or physically undertaken, for example by attending a public demonstration.

Quakers   A Christian group founded by George Fox in 1660.

Reconciliation   Repairing a broken relationship between two or more people.

Reparation   Making amends for any damage done.

Repent   To regret having done the wrong thing.

Restorative justice   A victim-focused form of justice. It aims to heal the harm caused by a crime in the best way for a victim and the community. It usually involves the victim and criminal meeting to consider the harm caused and the way to repair it.

Resurrection   Rising from the dead. Jesus was resurrected on the third day after his death by crucifixion.

Sacraments   A religious act believed to be a visible sign of God's grace or goodness to people.

Sanctions   Punishments imposed on a country or group because of non-observance of a law.

Sanctity of life   The belief that all life is holy because it is created by God.

Secular   Means worldly things and attitudes which are not regarded as religious or holy.

Slave trade   The buying and selling of people for use as slaves.

Subsidies   Government grants to provide economic support to various social groups, such as farmers.

Universal Declaration of Human Rights   A document of 30 articles that outlines the rights all humans should be entitled to.

Vatican   The independent state within the centre of Rome, Italy, that is the spiritual and organisational centre of the Catholic Church. The Pope lives here.

Vicar   The name for a minister in the Church of England.

Work ethic   Attitude towards work.

The wars illustrated on page 80 are (in order):
First World War (1914–18); Second World War (1939–45); Vietnam War (1962–75); Second Gulf War (2003).

Index